If this book inspired you, please share it with someone you want to inspire.

Conversations with a BILLIONAIRE

seize the **moment**
take a **leap**
the **world is waiting**

Ted W. Egly

This book is dedicated to my wife, Kathryn, who is a living example of unconditional love, encouragement, and support. And to our extraordinary and dynamic four sons (aka cowboys): George, Clark, Paul and Luke.

Contents

Preface

Years ago, I had a once-in-a-lifetime opportunity to work for someone whose board member was a billionaire. The Billionaire's last name is prominent in American history and culture.

I was privileged to be part of very enriching life and leadership lessons, conversations, meetings, and meals with this Billionaire over the course of several years.

Since I grew up in a family who loved history (my grandfather was an author and speaker on American history), I would ask the Billionaire questions regarding his memories of history and general questions about his life. I was, and am, an incurable learner with insatiable curiosity. What I found...beneath all the grandiosity of the multi-million-dollar homes, the glamor, the high-life and the power... was a human being who struggled with things that you and I wrestle with in our everyday life and leadership: tough decisions, "what-if" moments, fears, challenges, and uncertainty.

I've captured some of the lessons I learned in my conversations with him and observations of him throughout the book along with other lessons that I've learned throughout my life.

The purpose of this book is to be a compass, not necessarily a map, to inspire you, to provide tools for your personal growth and to challenge your thinking and mindset. Inspiring you not to settle for mediocrity. Your worth and life have something of value and by holding back that value, you are robbing humanity of your gifts and talents. I believe that everyone needs a compelling future. Something to move towards...and if you're not moving towards something then many times you mistakenly settle for the current state. My hope is that with this book I help you move towards something compelling in your life.

Chapter 1
Life is Movement

One of the greatest lessons of all that I learned (or had reinforced) was the importance of reflecting on life's important moments and deciding the type of legacy I want to leave. One day we were sitting in one of the rooms, surrounded by European art, beautiful, fresh roses placed in expensive vases...the Billionaire was rather quiet that day, more than normal, when all of a sudden, he began crying. After a long and almost awkward silence, he said, "I have been blessed with so many resources. I wish I knew then what I know now. I would have been more generous with the resources I've been given. I wish I had done more for others." Watching tears running down his face, I saw a man whose humility resonated with me and still does to this day.

Though we may not have the same resources at our fingertips, we have resources. Resources that will enrich our teams, our families, our companies, and our communities. Resources that will be the catalyst of hope and courage to those in our sphere of influence. Those resources are found in a generous life: a life that is poured out in helping others succeed, to be their best, and become extraordinarily great.

Something I learned from being part of conversations with the

Billionaire is that you don't have to be a billionaire to make a difference. To begin, to start, to make forward motion toward making an impact on the world around you—be it small or large—just start. No matter who you are, or what your income may be, you can be remembered for doing great work, for adding value to the lives of others, you, too, can leave a legacy.

JUST START

*"There are two mistakes one can make along the road of truth.
Not going all the way, and not starting."*
~ Siddhartha Gautama

In 1687, Sir Isaac Newton published his pioneering book, *The Principia: Mathematical Principles of Natural Philosophy*, which outlined his three laws of motion. One of the laws Newton outlined has application across the landscape of your life: It's the first law of motion:

An object either remains at rest or continues to move at a constant velocity, unless acted upon by an external force. (i.e., Objects in motion tend to stay in motion. Objects at rest tend to stay at rest.)

Objects in motion tend to stay in motion.

The most important thing is to find a way to get started. Just start. When can you start? Soon is not as good as now.

Get used to starting.

Starting can be hard. Making a difference can be hard.

A while ago I suggested to someone who wanted to write a book to start by setting up a blog and starting to write. He responded, "I want to make sure I have enough content before I start writing."

Four years later. Nothing. Nada.

I can illustrate that scenario in other areas (work out more, become a better photographer, get certified in project management) many times over.

Translation. We would rather dream about doing something than actually take action.

Don't let that describe you.

In short: Start. Start now!

Author Seth Godin says risk is avoided because we've been trained to avoid failure. He defines anxiety as experiencing failure in advance.

Consider the state of the rest of the world. If your project doesn't have forward movement, then compared to the rest of the world, you're actually moving backward. As Godin says, *"Like a rock in a flowing river, you might be standing still, but given the movement around you, collisions are inevitable."*

Godin suggests that the paradox for the person who favors no movement is that there's far less instability around the log floating down the same river. It's moving forward, it's changing, but related to the river around it, it's comparatively calm.

You could be wrong

One of the voices, lines of dialogue, that fear uses is the word "no." Or another go-to phrase that fear enjoys so much is the phrase "you could be wrong."

Fear is like the character that keeps stumbling into the play of your life. Fear keeps barging into the door onto the stage. (Even though the character, fear, isn't included in the plot.) Characters in the play are trying to move the plot forward. And fear tries to interrupt the play and say, "You could be wrong," thus interrupting the narrative, causing the plot not to unfold as it should.

That is correct. You could be wrong. Silence fear and acknowledge "Yes, that is correct. I could be wrong. And if I am, I will have the opportunity to learn something."

It turns out that the original Starbucks didn't sell brewed coffee.

That's right. They sold coffee beans and tea leaves and even spices.

Starbucks was wrong.

Some believe that the original owners of Starbucks made a blunder. They were more focused on selling beans and didn't sell brewed coffee. Had they just continued down the path of selling beans, Starbucks would not have succeeded. It took Howard Schultz, a trip to Italy, and his absolute fascination and obsession with espresso to turn Starbucks into what we know of it today. Now there are more than 20,000 Starbucks around the world.

Here's the point. Can you imagine if the *wrong* Starbucks had never been designed and constructed? What if they said, "Well, we're not sure if this bean thing is going to work, so let's sit on our hands and do NOTHING?"

Starbucks isn't alone:

- William Wrigley Jr. sold soap and baking powder and stumbled on the value of gum while giving it away for free. The gum proved to be more popular than his actual product. Wrigley went on to manufacture his own chewing gum brand and today the company makes billions in revenue and is one of the most recognizable brands in America.

- Instagram originally started as Burbn, a check-in app that included gaming and photo elements. The creators of Burbn were concerned that there was too much clutter and they'd never gain traction in the marketplace so they took away all the elements except photos. They built an app that focused solely on photography and it's been growing in popularity steadily since it first debuted in 2010.

- Twitter started as Odeo, which was a network where people could find and subscribe to podcasts; however, they ended up moving toward a drastic change focused on a micro-blogging platform. It's now one of the most popular mobile social networking apps in the United States.

Initiative and starting are about "let's see" and "I'll try."

Perhaps the thing you should do is something new, especially if there's no clear right answer. Something new is often the right path when the world is complex.

And…you could be wrong, but start anyway.

Starting as a way of doing life

> *"What good is an idea if it remains an idea?*
> *Try. Experiment. Iterate.*
> *Fail. Try again. Change the world."*
> ~ Simon Sinek

Maybe the answer is not try "harder," but try "different."

Innovation can be an enigma. Inspiration is generally random. But it's understandable from all the success you see in the marketplace that you can rise to the occasion and create innovative solutions.

Allow the habit to be ingrained and become a starter. You will then begin to find more and more things to notice, to instigate and initiate.

Forward motion is a strong asset.

Life is movement

I believe that life without change is death. Consider the human body, which comprises, on average, one hundred trillion cells. Every cell is continuously in motion: *transforming, replenishing, preserving, and growing.* Thus, I believe life is about movement, and movement is life.

Human beings have a spirit that hungers for growth and movement.

Perfect will never arrive. The perfect time never arrives. Don't let yourself off the hook making excuses to not move forward. It's your responsibility. You're always too old or too young or under-funded or uneducated or busy or something.

Every day you have a choice to start, to move forward, to change. Or you can cling to destructive routines and habits, continuing on in the moments of dullness in a steady march to obscurity and death.

"Life should not be a journey to the grave with the intention of arriving safely in a pretty and well preserved body, but rather to skid in broadside in a cloud of smoke, thoroughly used up, totally worn out, and loudly proclaiming 'Wow! What a Ride!'"
~ Hunter S. Thompson

Use your time wisely. Explore. Create. Start. Move forward.

Throw a pebble

You don't know where the ripples are going to go when you throw a pebble in the water of starting. The real question is, "are you going to throw it?"

People get trapped with being too safe. You can't get off the starting block because you're worried about being judged or criticized. The worst effect is NOT being judged and criticized. It's people having no opinion whatsoever on what you do. That's creative death.

People who feel threatened will always try to bring you down.

Haters are not your problem. Obscurity is your problem. Don't be indifferent.

The people who succeed are those who silence the voices of the inner critic and ignore the external ones.

"The way to get started is to quit talking and begin doing."
~ Walt Disney

Seize the Moment: Take the Leap

"Come to the edge, He said.
They said: We are afraid.
Come to the edge, He said.
They came. He pushed them,
And they flew…"
~ Guillaume Apollinaire

In 2015 my family took a vacation to Colorado. We experienced the spectacular mountainous views that words can't properly be etched to describe such beauty. The days exploring were filled with wonder, adventure, and risk (particularly for my four boys, aka cowboys). One day we visited the Garden of the Gods in Colorado Springs. My boys were elated to climb the rock formations. My older son, George, scaled the jagged formations then took a "leap" into my arms.

Little did we know at the time that we would be walking to the edge in the coming weeks, seizing the moment and taking a leap by uprooting from our 13 years of living in the Chicago area…and moving to Colorado.

We left a familiar place and adventured to a world of new possibility at a new location. We left a strong community of people we love so much and moved toward building a new community and new relationships. I left a well-established job and started a new one filled with many new opportunities for growth and development.

We seized the moment and took the leap.

Isn't that what life should be about? Embracing life with a desire for adventure and eyes of wonder? Aren't you designed to make a dent in the universe and leave your mark?

Move from the mundane and live the extraordinary

"One life on this earth is all that we get, whether it is enough or not enough,

and the obvious conclusion would seem to be that at the very least we are fools if we do not live it as fully and bravely and beautifully as we can."
~Frederick Buechner

You are being called to move away from the mundane and live the extraordinary. Is your goal how long you live or that you live? The reality is that to do great work, you have to feel that you're making a difference and that you're a part of something significant.

You are being called out to not just exist but to really LIVE!

Cooper (played by Matthew McCaughey) in the movie *Interstellar* said it so well, "It's like we've forgotten who we are—explorers, pioneers, not caretakers… We used to look up at the sky and wonder at our place in the stars. Now we just look down and worry about our place in the dirt."

How are you moving away from the mundane and the comfort of staying invisible?

We can become boring for the purpose of evading any potential dangers and hide in the backdrop of life and be invisible. It is much easier to hide, isn't it? Oh, there are other words for hiddenness—average, mediocre, invisible, normal, compliant, predictable, safe—and the list could go on.

You were not born to be a person who lives a life of average. Many of us choose to live a life of mediocrity and find ourselves in danger of vanishing into the chasm of average and safe.

How have you been hiding these days? Who has missed out on the gifts you were made to share with the world? How can you move away from mediocrity? Learn a new skill! Start that project you've been putting off! Make that job move! Build a new relationship!

Each moment carries within it a decision point and the capacity to shape a lifetime. And this is the challenge that comes in those moments: the greater that moment's opportunity, the greater the decision point and risk required. Whenever you choose to take a leap, you move from hiding to visibility.

Unlock today's potential by choice

"Faith is taking the first step even when you don't see the whole staircase."
~ Martin Luther King, Jr.

The budding potential of a moment is unlocked by the choices you make. If a moment is the gate through which your journey begins, then choice is the key that unlocks the adventure. The most powerful activity you will engage in today is making choices.

Sometimes it feels as if life is nothing more than dull, that there isn't anything there to seize. That is the greatest tragedy of all.

Many times we can be captivated by others' lives. Envying them, even. One of the mistakes we can make is concluding that those on the other side of the curtain are more talented, more gifted, or just more fortunate than we are. We assume that they must be different from us; otherwise, we would be living that kind of life too.

Let's be honest: Simply watching life go by will never yield deep satisfaction. You cannot live vicariously through someone else's life. You were not designed to gaze from the sidelines. Quit making excuses that it's about talent or giftedness or intelligence; it's about moving out of passivity into activity.

It's not how long you live, but THAT you live

"People are always getting ready to live, but never live."
~ Emerson

Make a connection.
Make a difference.
Choose to live.
It's YOUR turn to stand up and stand out.

> *"It is nothing to die. It is an awful thing never to have lived."*
> ~Jean Valjean, Les Miserables

It's seldom a deliberate action to choose to exist rather than to live. For most of us, we are simply rocked to sleep. But there is no rest in this condition. To slumber and sleep through your dreams is acquiescing to a life of restless nights and unfulfilled days. To avoid the discomfort of fear, doubt, and disappointment, we have deadened ourselves from the exhilaration of a life fully lived.

We all can be troubled by the fear of living lives of insignificance. Somehow we all recognize that to play it safe is to lose the game. By definition, an adventure is "an unusual and exciting, typically hazardous, experience or activity." In other words, it can come at great risk and significant cost.

You were created for significance and purpose.

If we are going to seize this moment and take a leap, then we must accept the reality that we have no control over countless things. We have zero control over when we die or how we die. Instead, we must take full responsibility for what we do have control over—HOW we choose to live.

Take the leap.

You never failed without risking so take the leap

No matter what kind of life you've lived up to this point in time, no matter how many countless wrong choices you've made, the next moment in time is waiting to give birth to new life.

Fear may be staring you down. Fear of failing.

If you have never failed, then there is a high probability that you have never risked. The truth is, you cannot fail without risking.

It is not a platitude to say that the path to greatness is paved by failure.

Face your fear. Lean in.

When we face our fears, we look straight into the eyes of opportunity, and the courage we frequently need to engage our ultimate challenge can be found *only* in the midst of engaging the challenge. There is a point as we take a leap and lean into making a dent in the universe that a battle begins. It is at this point where we experience conflict, opposition, and resistance. But it is also where we have the ultimate opportunity.

You are not called to live a low-risk life. You are called not to be a survivor, but to be a conqueror and thrive.

Meaningful adventure: it's your move

The journey begins when you choose. Stop wasting time. Choose a life of meaningful adventure. When you do, you will live in an epicenter of possibilities.

The most significant moments to seize are the ones that do not come easily.

Life has many places we can get away to and hide, places that can make us feel safe and secure. Take no action. Make no significant move or contribution. Allow us to avoid the doors and places that yield uncertainty. Are we afraid to go through a door that may yield uncertainty? Is it possible that we, too, are afraid to go out a different door? The reality is that the new way out is packed full with uncertainty but with that uncertainty comes mystery, adventure, and wonder.

Seize the moment. The world is waiting.

Stop waiting for passion

People read stories about successful business professionals or leaders or artists or entrepreneurs and (wrongly) assume that once they chose their field, they woke up every morning supported by huge reservoirs of energy for their work. The pressure around this is equivalent to the idea that there is one perfect soulmate out there in the world for you to marry, and if you don't find him or her, you're doomed to relational discontent.

No one's life is like that!

Thomas Edison said it best: "Genius is one percent inspiration, and ninety-nine percent perspiration." And in the same way, life is much like that.

The indispensable truth of the soul is to believe in the significance of our contributions. But to believe that choosing the right, perfect path will usher in a nonstop tsunami of motivation is an illusion that will leave us frustrated and drive us mad.

Many of us wait for passion to lead us somewhere we're not. Instead, start by bringing passion to the place where you are.

Just start

Quit waiting to start. Start something, now. Today.

Start a project, create a brand, make a commotion, take a risk.

Not just, "I will start one day," or "I'm considering starting something," or, "I'm going to have another brain storming session, then start," or, "I'm going to have one more meeting before starting…"

No, actually start. Go beyond the point of no return.

Leap.

Dive in.

Commit.

Make something happen.

"Imperfect action is better than perfect inaction"
~ President Harry S. Truman

Just start!

CALL TO ACTION

What is the one project you've been meaning to start? Commit to yourself and someone you trust (as a point of accountability) that you will start this week.

LEADERSHIP IS EVERYBODY'S CHALLENGE, AND IT STARTS — WITH —

YOU!

Chapter 2
Start with You

I recall a particular conversation one afternoon where the Billionaire and other guests talked about the recent news of a senior leader being asked to step down from an organization. One reason, along with others, was this leader was creating a toxic culture. As a result, this person was no longer looking out for the team, the organization, or the best interest of others. Only himself.

Reflecting back, even now, I vividly recall the conversation and sum up that the executive leader didn't lead himself well. He wasn't teachable. He wasn't humble. He led himself poorly. Leadership isn't a right; it's a responsibility. And the responsibility starts with leading yourself well.

Remaining Teachable:
The Never-Ending Path to Wisdom

"The most difficult subjects can be explained to the most slow-witted man if he has not formed any idea of them already; but the simplest thing cannot be made clear to the most intelligent man if he is firmly persuaded that he knows already."

~ Leo Tolstoy

Can you remember a time when you were firmly persuaded about something? Maybe that which you were firmly persuaded about impacted your ability to listen to someone else's point of view. The type of firm persuasion that Tolstoy suggests can limit us from receiving feedback and seeking input, ultimately preventing us from becoming better leaders and professionals.

There was an article written about the former Chicago Bulls player, Derrick Rose, during the time he received the NBA's MVP award. The article contained encouraging words of congratulations from his teammates and one from NBA legend Michael Jordan. One comment in the article spoke volumes about Rose's leadership. His teammate said:

> *He's humble, he's coachable. It doesn't matter if the 12th man on the team says something to him, he's going to look you in the eye and listen to you and nod his head and try to do it better...that's just the kind of guy he is. And that is so rare. That is so rare. He's got great people around him, coaching him, and helping him out.*

We could learn something from Rose. We may never receive the fame and fortune of Rose, but we do have something in common with him, and that is the choice to be teachable. When we are teachable, we are *attentive, curious, receptive, trusting, and shapeable.*

Leadership guru John Maxwell recommends we ask ourselves these questions to determine our level of *teachability:*

- Do I listen more than I talk?
- Am I open to changing my opinion based on new information?
- Do I readily admit when I am wrong?
- Do I observe before acting on a situation?
- Do I ask questions?
- Am I willing to ask a question that will expose my ignorance?
- Am I open to other people's ideas?
- Am I open to doing things in a way I haven't done before?
- Am I willing to ask for directions?

• Do I act defensive when criticized, or do I listen openly for truth?

A teachable attitude is a never-ending path to wisdom. The brilliant essayist, E.B. White, suggests that, *"There is a bright future for complexity, what with one thing always leading to another."*

E.B. White distills in his statement of complexity that there is ALWAYS something new to learn. When we discover something new and give it a tug, we find it inexorably leads us to another discovery and then another. The sensational desire for curiosity and learning is the path to wisdom.

Think about it this way: The ability to learn is a defining characteristic of being human. The ability to continue to learn, or remain teachable, is a crucial skill of leadership and in life. The reality is that when any of us loses that ability, we no longer grow.

CALL TO ACTION

How about giving teachability a shot today? When was the last time you did something for the first time? When was the last time you were vulnerable by diving into something about which you were not the expert? Will you take on a teachable attitude this week and venture down the path of never-ending wisdom?

LEADERSHIP BEGINS WITH YOU

"Nothing so conclusively proves a man's ability to lead others, as what he does from day to day to lead himself."
~ Thomas J. Watson

Many well-known thought leaders of our day suggest that one's energy should largely be allocated to investing in and leading *self*.

The author, founder, and former CEO of Visa Card, Dee Hock, who is considered by many to be an exemplary model and teacher on leadership, suggests that leaders need to analyze how much time and energy they devote to leading those below them, over them (vertically), their peers (horizontally), and themselves.

Hock's suggestion is that leaders should invest *fifty percent* of their focus on *self-leadership*, and the remaining fifty percent in leading others. Maximizing self-leadership requires self-awareness and introspection, and ultimately transforming the lens through which you see the world around you.

Below are indicators that we're not being intentional about self-leadership.

- Not practicing self-awareness
- Making everything about us
- Procrastinating instead of taking action
- Judging quickly, instead of suspending judgment
- Camping out in the arena of self-doubt, instead of self-worth
- Becoming self-righteous, instead of putting ego at bay
- Allowing fear to keep us from our highest potential

How are you doing these days with leading self?

Strive to be "others-centered"

"Really believe in your heart of hearts that your fundamental purpose, the reason for being, is to enlarge the lives of others. Your life will be enlarged also. And all of the other things we have been taught to concentrate on will take care of themselves."
~ Pete Thigpen

Leading self requires that you make it about *others*. Your success as a leader happens, in part, when you are "others-centered."

A big part of leadership is that you constantly have to remind yourself that it ISN'T about you. It's about others. It's about serving the mission of the organization.

In my early 20s I worked in Europe, and throughout my time there I would tour ornate castles and beautiful landmarks. One landmark I visited was a 14th century church in Italy where our guide was a lovely elderly nun, with infectious energy and an engaging personality. After the tour I commented about how much I appreciated her energy and focused interest in us.

What she said to me next (in broken English) has resonated with me to this day. She said, *"When I walk into a room, it's not 'here I AM,' it's 'there YOU are.'"* It's not about me. It's about others.

Are you a thermometer or a thermostat?

You are either a thermometer or a thermostat. You will either react to and reflect the climate around you, or you will set the climate around yourself. You set the tone for others. A thermometer will communicate to you what the temperature currently is, as it simply *reacts* to external factors. A thermostat can be deliberately set and dictates the temperature. In short, it *regulates* the environment.

Avoid approval addiction

One of the challenges of leading self can be the unhealthy desire to seek approval from others. This can derail us from being our authentic self. It causes us to become masters in the art of *impression management*. Approval Addiction pulls us in.

The reality is that we are not the passive victims of others' opinions. Their opinions are powerless until we validate them. The reality is that no one's approval will impact us unless we grant it credibility.

> *"No one can make you feel inferior without your consent."*
> ~ Eleanor Roosevelt

Leading self requires a healthy balance of authenticity, while managing the temptation to cross the line into approval addiction (which we will talk more about in chapter 6).

Focus on making a difference

"Leadership is not about titles, positions, or flow charts. It is about one life influencing another."
~ John Maxwell

Intentional self-leadership requires us to put more focus on what we are FOR (making a difference) than what we are AGAINST (trying to be right or just make a point).

For instance, telling somebody they are wrong is not the same thing as leading them and *inspiring* them to do what's right. We shouldn't be content with just pointing out what others are doing wrong. Instead, our role is to *inspire* people to do what's right.

Let's be honest: We all want to make a difference…and not just for ourselves. At the end of our lives, we want someone to say, *"My life is a little fuller and richer, my world is a little bigger, I'm a better human being because THIS person walked the planet."*

CALL TO ACTION

I dare you. Wake up tomorrow morning and ask this adventurous question, "What can I do today to make a difference in the world?"

Know thyself

There's a crisis in self-leadership, and that's identity crisis. It happens when we wrap our identity around an outcome, event, and/or title/role.

For example, some psychologists indicate that one of the most important aspects to any high performance is the ability to *separate one's personhood from any particular result.* Similarly, effective leaders are greater than any individual outcome. Their sense of self-worth is separate from "the deal."

Don't get me wrong. That doesn't mean we take a laissez-faire approach to our work. It simply means that we separate our worth from the outcome. Self-leadership, in this case, means our value and worth are *not* tied to a particular outcome.

Treasure your time, eliminate hurry

> *"Until you value yourself, you won't value your time."*
> ~ Scott Peck

The American cardiologist, Meyer Friedman, coined the phrase "hurry sickness." He defines it as *"above all, a continuous struggle and unremitting attempt to accomplish or achieve more and more things or participate in more and more events in less and less time, frequently in the face of opposition, real or imagined, from other persons."*

Leading self requires that we properly align our priorities and treasure our time, or someone else will. We must be ruthless in setting up the appropriate boundaries to ensure others aren't dictating our priorities. Those we care for the most deserve our best.

Leadership is everybody's challenge, and it starts with YOU

Leadership is everybody's challenge. That's right. That includes YOU.

Remember that leading is a skill, not a gift. You are not born with it; you learn how to lead.

As Kouzes and Posner said, in *The Leadership Challenge*, "The next time you say to yourself, 'Why don't they do something about this?' look in this mirror. Ask the person you see, 'Why don't you do something about this?' "

That means, at times, challenging the status quo. Challenging mindsets and ways of thinking. Its leaders mandate to challenge the status quo, to challenge the process…to point people toward a preferred future.

CALL TO ACTION

This week, how will you be more purposeful about self-leadership? Here are some things to consider when leading self this week: (NOTE: All of these are calls YOU make, and when you add them up, they create your life.)

- What will you feed your mind?
- What thoughts will you dwell on?
- Who will you allow to influence your inner life and choices?
- How will you spend your time?

BACK TO THE BASICS

In 1959, legendary coach Vince Lombardi took over the Green Bay Packers on the heels of a demoralizing year, where the Packers finished the season with one win and ten losses. To top it off, the Packer franchise had a string of almost ten *years* of losses.

What set Lombardi apart wasn't necessarily just tweaking the already existing plays, giving an inspirational speech, or bringing in top-notch talent. Instead, he brought the players *back to the basics*. What Lombardi did was unorthodox, but later many considered BRILLIANT!

Lombardi said to his players during a practice one day, *"Everybody stop and gather around."* Kneeling down and grabbing the football, he said, *"Let's start at the beginning. This is a football. These are the yard markers. I'm the coach. You are the players."* He started with the basics.

The statement, although elementary, *"This is a football"* is a simple reminder to not lose sight of the fundamentals. One of the cornerstones of being part of a winning organization is coming *back to the basics*.

James Kouzes and Barry Posner's book, *The Truth About Leadership*, identifies 10 fundamental truths about leadership, and focuses on leadership effectiveness by getting back to the basics.

Here are Kouzes and Posner's *Ten Truths about Leadership*:

1. You Make a Difference
   - It starts with believing in yourself.
   - You can make a positive impact.

2. Credibility Is the Foundation of Leadership
   - If you don't believe in yourself, nobody else will.
   - People will not willingly follow those who are not credible.

3. Values-Driven Commitment
   - Know what you stand for, and understand the values of others.
   - It's hard to commit to something that doesn't fit with who you are.

4. Focusing on the Future Sets Leaders Apart
   - Gain perspective from the past, but look to the future.
   - Leaders are custodians of the future.

5. You Can't Do It Alone
   - Leadership is a team sport.
   - Be devoted to what is best for others.

6. Trust Rules
   - Trust is the glue that holds teams together.
   - You must give trust to earn trust.

7. Challenge is the Crucible for Greatness
   - Great achievements don't happen when you keep things the same.
   - Change involves challenge, and challenge tests you.

8. You Either Lead by Example or You Don't Lead at All
   - Model the way and keep your promises.
   - Be willing to admit mistakes, and learn from them.

9. The Best Leaders are the Best Learners
- Be an improvement fanatic.
- Learning takes time, attention, practice and feedback.

10. Leadership is an Affair of the Heart
- Leaders are in love with their customers, clients, and their mission.
- Leaders make others feel important.

These fundamentals are examples that can facilitate the trajectory for future accomplishments. Like Lombardi, who brought a failing organization back to the basics of football by grabbing a pigskin and saying "this is a football," how might it help our leadership if we took a few minutes each day to focus on the basics?

Journeying back to the basics is a golden opportunity. It orients us toward intentional leadership, providing growth and development.

Triumph Ist Possible

Chapter 3
Triumph is Possible

Like the Billionaire, we all have moments of greatness, moments where we are leading teams with zeal and operating at our zenith potential. There are also those moments where things are less than stellar. There will be moments where you're faced with tough decisions or seemingly insurmountable adversity, and moments where you feel alone.

The Billionaire was a man whose leadership evolved over the years as a result of reflecting on past mistakes (adversity and setbacks), past decisions, and past challenges. He didn't allow moments of adversity to define his life. Instead, he chose to think about adversity, and how it shaped him, differently.

Though you may not be a billionaire, you are a leader. We are ALL leaders. Your leadership is your sphere of influence. Whether you are a stay-at-home parent, a coach, a teacher, or an executive, it's critical to reflect on your decisions and the value you are adding to your cause, your home life, your initiative, your organization, your teams, and to others in your life.

As a leader, you have a choice as to how you will show up amidst the backdrop of adversity.

ADVERSITY, CHALLENGE, AND TRIUMPH

"All the adversity I've had in my life, all my troubles and obstacles, have strengthened me..."
~ Walt Disney

We all face adversity and challenges. It comes as a result of...well, being human. Sometimes we seek a challenge, and other times it seeks us.

I've experienced trials, as well as triumph, I've faced battles related to health problems, injury, career transitions, and the loss of support systems, which have all shaped the person I am today.

What I've learned is that my *reaction* determines how successful I am in conquering and even thriving through difficulty!

- You can see a disaster or opportunity.
- You can be blinded by success, or stay objective.
- You can lose control, or choose to remain calm.

Desperation. Hopelessness. Fear. Powerlessness. There is absolutely nothing that *makes* us feel this way. We CHOOSE to give in to such feelings. We can choose to be blindly led by our lizard brain, or we can understand our feelings and learn to filter them.

HOW you respond to adversity, challenges, and problems... MATTERS

"By acting as if I was not afraid I gradually ceased to be afraid."
~ Theodore Roosevelt

How we respond to the challenges, trials, and obstacles in life is up to us. We CAN choose to be calm through life's ups and downs.

Researchers have looked at what enables some people to endure adversity, challenges, and even suffering. The focus has moved over the last decade from looking only at how some people make it through adversity, to how some people actually come out *stronger* than before. Just as there is a condition called "post-traumatic stress disorder," researchers are now talking about "post-traumatic growth."

What researchers have found is that not only can adversity lead to growth, growth cannot be attained without adversity!

Here are some BENEFITS to adversity:

1. When you rise to a challenge, you find it reveals capabilities and a capacity within you that would have otherwise remained dormant.
   - You discover very quickly what you are really made of.
   - You won't always be able to dictate the outcome you want. Instead, you can ask yourself, "How would the person I most want to BE show up and act in this situation?"

2. Adversity can strengthen relationships and change your priorities toward what's most important.
   - One of the most common results of people who go through adversity is that they come to have a more profound appreciation for other people.
   - Adversity causes you to favor *relationships* over "things."

Resilient, adaptable, and unflappable coolness

We need to have "unflappable coolness" amidst the pressures of life.

Yes. It's possible.

Life can shake you at times. People will upset you. Situations are going to happen that catch you off guard, intimidate, or even scare you. Surprises are guaranteed. There will be times you will feel overwhelmed and not ready to face the challenge in front of you. In this midst of these situations, grace and composure are two characteristics you can adopt.

Ryan Holiday outlines this brilliantly in his book, *The Obstacle is the Way*, by sharing the story of John D. Rockefeller and how he was able to remain calm amidst the storms of life.

> *But even as a young man, Rockefeller had sangfroid: unflappable coolness under pressure. He could keep his head while he was losing his shirt. Better yet, he kept his head while everyone else lost theirs.*
>
> *…Rockefeller's personality: resilient, adaptable, calm, brilliant. He could not be rattled—not by economic crisis, not by a glittery mirage of false opportunities, not by aggressive, bulling enemies, not even by federal prosecutors. …was he born this way? No. This was learned behavior.*

You read that correctly. Unflappable coolness can be learned.

Adaptive capacity

You can choose to increase your capacity to adapt and be flexible when adversity and obstacles stand in your way.

Do you currently face any problems or challenges in your life?

The truth is all of us have dealt with or are dealing with problems. The problem fairy is an Equal Opportunity Distributor. He is all over the globe today!

Nobody…nobody…gets beyond the reach of problems.

We can stop seeing the "problems" in front of us as problems. We can reframe them.

> *"If you can change your circumstances, do something about it. If you can't change your circumstances, change your perspective."*
> ~ Craig Groeschel

In the book *Geeks and Geezers*, Warren Bennis and Robert Thomas reveal an extensive study on emerging and tenured leaders. Their research suggests that one of the strongest qualities that determines success is the quality of *adaptive capacity*.

They define adaptive capacity as:

Applied creativity. It is the ability to look at problems or crisis and see an array of unconventional solutions.

Adaptive capacity allows an individual to confront unfamiliar situations with gusto, confidence, and unbridled optimism. Why? They are not paralyzed by fear or discouraged by anxiety in difficult situations.

CALL TO ACTION

What problems bring you the biggest concern these days? What is it exactly that you are afraid might happen as a result of this problem? How, with regard to this particular problem, could you move toward having more resiliency and adaptive capacity?

Grit

It takes determination and strength to deal with the adversities of life. Don't allow the setbacks to get you down or the roadblocks to deter you from your goals. Don't become discouraged when things don't go according to plan.

Science has found that the most successful people are not necessarily the most intelligent or the most talented, but rather the ones who have grit—the ones who can tough it out. It's that determination of spirit, that steadfast courage, that is essential in dealing with challenges.

Angela L. Duckworth, PhD, a University of Pennsylvania researcher, defines grit as "perseverance and passion for long-term goals." She explains:

Grit entails working strenuously toward challenges, maintaining effort and interest over years despite failure, adversity, and plateaus in progress. The gritty individual approaches achievement as a marathon; his or her advantage is stamina.

Being gritty matters. Pushing through the mire of adversity matters more than talent and more than having a high IQ.

People with grit are more likely to achieve positive outcomes.

Adversity—an open door or a brick wall?

"Everyone can make a difference if she or he dares to step out to seize the opportunity and take the initiative."
~ Unknown

Adversity is not just something that happens "to" you, but something you can also look for, for the purpose of testing your limits, and for your own personal growth and development.

I'm reminded of Randy Pausch, who delivered his now-famous "last lecture" at Carnegie Mellon University. In his message, Randy, said:

"The brick walls are there for a reason. They're not there to keep us out. The brick walls are there to give us a chance to show how badly we want something."

How do we challenge ourselves? How do we seek out adversity? Here are some suggestions:

- Starting a business
- Trying a new creative approach in your business
- Getting in better physical shape
- Going back to school or taking a course online, for the purpose of building a new skill
- Repairing a damaged relationship
- Taking a step forward on something you've been avoiding

What might seem like a brick wall could simply be a door to a new future asking: "What do you want?" and "How badly do you want it?"

Choose to see open doors while others see brick walls. Seize the opportunities that conceal themselves inside adversity, challenge, and obstacles. Take the initiative to move things forward.

Who will you become as a result of adversity?

> *"You are the storyteller of your own life,*
> *and you can create your own legend or not."*
> ~ Isabel Allende

Adversity causes you to come face-to-face with your inner self. It reminds you of what's important, what you value, and where you want to go.

Going into battle, overcoming fears, and entering territory laced with unknowns allows YOU to create a narrative. You can tell the story of how you were challenged, met that challenge, and became a new and better self.

Overcoming one obstacle says you're worthy of more. Each adverse moment reveals an opportunity to develop, grow, and triumph. It allows you to demonstrate that you have what it takes and that you will forge ahead with grit and creativity.

Smile in the face of adversity and any obstacle that life lobs at you (or that you seek) by improving in spite of it, and because of it.

In the 1940s, a brilliant doctor named Viktor Frankl was imprisoned in a concentration camp. They confiscated his possessions, took away his livelihood, scorned him, and executed his family. They restricted him to a cell with no way to escape his circumstances. However, in spite of this, he states:

> *Everything can be taken from a man but one thing: the last of the human freedoms—to choose one's attitude in any given set of circumstances, to choose one's own way.*

We are all going to face problems and setbacks. The solution is not to avoid problems. Quite the contrary! We need the character to forge ahead. Our growth is dependent on how we face those problems. Growth is not the ability to avoid problems. Instead, growth is the ability to handle larger and more interesting problems.

Life is a process of overcoming barriers—a string of fortified boundaries and limits that we must transcend. Each time you'll learn something. Each time you'll develop wisdom, discernment, strength, and a new outlook. Each time, fear and doubt fall away, until all that is left is you: THE BEST version of you.

"I must not fear. Fear is the mind-killer. Fear is the little-death that brings total obliteration. I will face my fear. I will permit it to pass over me and through me. And when it has gone past I will turn the inner eye to see its path. Where the fear has gone there will be nothing. Only I will remain."
~ Frank Herbert

Today, you can be eager, enthusiastic and cheerful…knowing that adversity will not get the best of you. You can be victorious and triumphant.

WILL YOU RING THE BELL AND QUIT?

"Success seems to be connected with action. Successful people keep moving. They make mistakes, but they don't quit."
~ Conrad Hilton

Author Steven Pressfield writes about the rigorous training of the Navy SEALS. He identifies how the SEALS separate those who quit the training from those who triumph and succeed.
Pressfield says:

> *Navy SEAL training puts its candidates through probably the most intense physical ordeal in the US military. The reason is that they're trying to break*

you. SEAL trainers want to see if the candidate will crack. Better that
the aspiring warrior fails here—at Coronado Island in San Diego—than
someplace where a real wartime mission and real lives are at stake.

In SEAL training they have a bell. When a candidate can't take the agony
any longer—the 6-mile ocean swims or the 15-mile full-load runs or the
physical and mental ordeals on no sleep and no food…when he's had enough
and he's ready to quit, he walks up and rings the bell.

That's it. It's over.

They quit. They *ring* the bell.

I don't pretend to understand the mental anguish and physical
exertion of the Navy SEALS training. Can I suggest to you that each
of us has parameters set up in the caverns of our mind of when to
"ring the bell" and quit?

The reason quitting can be so easy at times is because we become
mentally defeated. Maybe it's when rejection, anxiety, or fear become
too much to bear.

Ultra-marathoner Dick Collins says, on persevering through difficult races:

Decide before the race the conditions that will cause you to stop and drop
out. You don't want to be out there saying, "Well gee, my leg hurts, I'm a
little dehydrated, I'm sleepy, I'm tired, and it's cold and windy." And talk
yourself into quitting. If you are making a decision based on how you feel at
that moment, you will probably make the wrong decision.

We have to decide now—before we go any further, before times get
any harder (and they will)—what we will endure and persist through.

Maybe we've quit in times past because of a failed project, bad
leadership decision, poorly executed crucial conversation, or whatever didn't work out like we expected.

To discover significance and strength in adversity differentiates
leaders from non-leaders. When one is tested and tried, or when
bad things happen, some people might feel isolated and powerless.

Leaders (that's YOU) find purpose and resolve.

Here are three things to consider before you ring that bell:

Lean into the crucible

> *"Experience is not what happens to a man.*
> *It is what a man does with what happens to him."*
> ~ Aldous Huxley

As leaders, we all undergo testing. I'm sure that each of you could personally share triumphant stories of emerging stronger, with lessons learned and tools to lead. Warren Bennis coined the word crucible: *"how individuals make meaning out of often difficult events and how that process of 'meaning-making' both galvanizes individuals and gives them their distinctive voice."*

Bennis says, *"The extraction of wisdom from the crucible experience is what distinguishes our successful leaders from those who are broken or burnt out by comparable experiences."*

The reality is that tests and challenges are the crucible for greatness. Challenges cause you to learn and grow.

Bennis says, *"The crucible is the occasion for real magic, the creation of something more valuable than any could imagine. In it, the individual is transformed, changed, created anew."*

Learn to adapt

> *"It is not the stress that kills us.*
> *It is effective adaption to stress that liberates us from the past."*
> ~ George Vaillant

Learning to adapt allows leaders to traverse more effectively through struggle, particularly in the crucible moments. They learn not to be DEFINED by difficulty.

Instead, they reflexively seek to understand the lesson and pick up new skills, which equip and empower them to move onto higher levels of achievement.

Harvard research found that leaders with adaptive capacity (referenced a few pages earlier) were continuing to learn new things, and looked forward with hope, eagerness, and optimism, instead of residing in the past.

Leverage courage

> *"Courage is rightly esteemed the first of human qualities...*
> *because it is the quality which guarantees all others."*
> ~ Winston Churchill

Today is jammed with new possibilities. One must cease meditating on the "would'ves, could'ves, and should'ves" of yesterday. Instead, what lurks at the doorway of your heart and knocks...is courage. Courage to move forward and see today as a new opportunity to do something great.

Action has magic in it.

You haven't quit and rung the bell today.

The path to courage is paved through a life of action and movement. Commit to MOVE forward with courage. Fear begets weakness, and courage begets strength. Imagine with me for a moment that there is a GATEKEEPER at the doorway of your heart, and that gatekeeper is courage. Your move: What will you choose to do?

CALL TO ACTION

What if today you chose to lean into whatever crucible you were facing with gusto? What if you were to choose to find meaning and purpose, and to seize the opportunity to adapt in spite of the hardship?

When our lives are filled with
expectations and possibility, we are
guided by faith and driven by hope to
do NOTHING less than create a
bright future.

Chapter 4
Bravery is a Choice

One particular night I was having dinner with the Billionaire, his family, and a couple of businessmen. One of the young businessmen had just lost a sizable amount of money in the stock market (it was the late '90s during the dot-com debacle). You could feel the stress in his voice, as the money he lost (which I will probably not see in my lifetime) had him discouraged, afraid, and disheartened.

Without skipping a beat, the Billionaire chuckled (at this time he was in his 80s) and said in his very deep, proper voice, "You better get used to uncertainty and troublesome times in your business. You will learn, as I have, to get up and try again."

If we are honest with ourselves, we will realize that we all make mistakes (hopefully not multi-million-dollar mistakes). The mistakes don't have to define our life, career, and leadership. Instead, allow those failures to be stepping-stones and learning opportunities for future success.

FAILURE IS NOT FINAL

"Success is not final, failure is not fatal: it is the courage to continue that counts."
~ Winston Churchill

1. Redefine failure

"My dad encouraged us to fail. Growing up, he would ask us what we failed at that week. If we didn't have something, he would be disappointed. It changed by mindset at an early age that failure is not the outcome, failure is not trying. Don't be afraid to fail."
~ Sara Blakely

How do you define failure?

What if your *definition* of failure is what is causing you to be paralyzed or stuck in that moment? Failure is not an event! It's a *judgment* about an event.

Remember, your identity is not tied to outcomes. Outcomes are separate from the person, and the people who execute the best are those who have an unwavering sense of self no matter what happens.

One of the greatest problems individuals have with failure is that they are too quick to judge unique circumstances in their lives and brand them as failures. Instead, they need to keep the bigger picture in mind.

Failure isn't negative

Failure can be a wonderful opportunity to grow and innovate. If you find that you are consistently getting angry with yourself, chances are slim that you will be able to *resurrect* anything from your experience. Your family, friends, colleagues, and those around you may lose that opportunity to grow as well.

Failure is an essential ingredient to learning and growth. The failure that occurs in your life doesn't shape you as much as *how* you respond to the failure does.

The worst failure is not in the event itself. The worst failure is to choose to remain paralyzed by it.

If we never have blunders or mistakes in our lives, then we are probably not making any decisions either. F. Scott Fitzgerald says something that pierces the heart, *"Never confuse a single mistake with a final mistake."*

Recently I came across an excerpt called *Rules for Being Human,* by Dr. Cherie Carter-Scott. Here are a few rules I believe describe the state we should be in:

Rule #1: You will learn lessons.

Rule #2: There are no mistakes – only lessons.

Rule #3: A lesson is repeated until it is learned.

Rule #4: If you don't learn the lessons, they get harder. (NOTE: Pain is one way the universe gets your attention.)

Rule #5: You'll know you've learned a lesson when your actions change.

Can you imagine Beethoven or Mozart trying to compose music so carefully that they never hit a wrong note? Do you believe that they would have been able to compose epic masterpieces if they completely avoided mistakes?

Beethoven was no stranger to mistakes, disappointments, and failure. In fact, at one point in his career his music teacher said he had no talent for music and "as a composer, he is hopeless."

Some other examples of those who failed, yet went on to succeed:

- 12 publishers rejected J.K. Rowling, the legendary author of the *Harry Potter* books, before selling her first book. Now she's worth more than $1 billion.
- Henry Ford went bankrupt multiple times before he experienced success.
- The California-born French chef, Julia Child, author and television celebrity, could barely cook until she was thirty-four years old.
- One of the greatest thinkers and brilliant minds of our time, Albert Einstein, was told by a schoolmaster in Munich that he

would "never amount to much."

- One of the most prolific inventors in history, Thomas Edison, was told as a youngster that he was not that bright.

All great successes persevere in the face of hardship, denial, and failings. They continue to believe in themselves and reject the idea that they are "failures."

As Elbert Hubbard said, "The greatest mistake you can make in life is to be continually fearing you will make one." A beneficial result to this might be, "If you want to be successful in life, continually fill your mind with opportunities, not obstacles, so that you will create them."

CALL TO ACTION

What's the one mistake or failure that haunts you? What trusted friend can you share it with as a step toward robbing it of its power?

---

2. Embrace failure as a teacher and a learning experience

"I've missed more than 9000 shots in my career. I've lost almost 300 games. 26 times, I've been trusted to take the game-winning shot and missed. I've failed over and over and over again in my life. And that is why I succeed."
~Michael Jordan

These words from the legendary Michael Jordan should echo in the chambers of our heart, filling them with hope and inspiration. Like Jordan and many other successful athletes, high-performing business leaders, and entrepreneurs, failure should be looked at with different lenses. How you view failure is a critical component to future success. Failure, in so many ways, is the fertilizer for future success.

If you can change the way you see failure, you gain the strength to keep charging ahead. Failure is the price you pay for *progress*. How do you view failure? Whether it be failure with a start-up, project, initiative, conversation, or some other avenue in which success was the hoped outcome…do you view it as an opportunity to grow, or do you see it as a stain on your credibility and as an absolute failure?

Many business professionals and leading psychologists of our day believe that failure (small and large) is necessary for growth. But it's "how" you view that failure that can set the trajectory of your future. Carol Dweck, a psychology professor at Stanford University, believes that what people believe (especially about failure) shapes the landscape of their life. She suggests that our "self-theories" dictate the interpretation of our experiences, and ultimately set the rhythm and boundaries of what we accomplish.

Think about it this way: If you don't put things in the right perspective, you'll focus on the extremes of success and failure and preoccupy yourself with a particular event.

Here's the deal. Every failure you encounter you face a fork in the road. You can give up or you can use it as an opportunity to learn from your missteps, take the right action, and begin again.

Freedom to fail
Some of the best organizations are the ones who don't penalize a person for making a mistake if that person used good judgment and was rational in his/her thinking. In contrast, there are times when failure was from not exercising the values of the organization, good judgment, and stewardship. In those times, the situation or decision is confronted and corrected.

"The better a person is, the more mistakes he will make, for the more new things he will try. I would never promote to a top-level job a man who was not making mistakes…otherwise he is sure to be mediocre."
~ Peter Drucker

After a mistake and failure, the *forces* of mediocrity will align to prevent you from proceeding. Keep your chin up when failure comes your way. Failure can be the fertilizer for future success. Fear of failure and risk aversion tethers you to limit your potential. Every failure you experience is an opportunity to take the appropriate action, learn from your mistakes, and start fresh.

> *"While one person hesitates because he feels inferior, the other is busy making mistakes and becoming superior."*
> ~ Henry Link

Failure is not final.

You must know WHO you are and FACE your shortcomings if you want to reach your full potential. That's right. You must face your shortcomings. You can't bury them and pretend that they don't exist. You must see yourself openly, admit your failures, shortcomings, and mistakes honestly, discover and embrace your strengths joyfully, and build on those strengths continually and passionately.

CALL TO ACTION

Are you allowing failure to be a stepping-stone instead of a stumbling block? How can you embrace a moment of failure as a springboard this week?

Failure should lead to learning

If failure does not lead to a new product, process, or discovery, it should lead to some type of learning. Leaders with developed character regarding failure have the poise to accept it without condemning themselves. Like a good football coach looking at the game films after the big loss, leaders review their failure with acceptance, but ask themselves and others, "What could we have done better? What was wrong in our analysis or system or process? What can we do to change?"

"Failure should be our teacher, not our undertaker. Failure is delay, not defeat. It is a temporary detour, not a dead end. Failure is something we can avoid only by saying nothing, doing nothing, and being nothing."

~ Denis Waitley

Here's the deal about winning and losing. The difference between winners and losers is that winners lose well (and learn from it), and losers lose poorly (don't learn from it, and stay stuck in self-pity). As a result, winners lose less in the future and do not lose the same way they lost last time, because they have learned from the loss and did not repeat the pattern.

Losers are more inclined to carry that losing pattern into the next endeavor, job, or relationship, and repeat the same way of losing.

When you lose, because you will at some point (if you haven't already)…sit with it, understand it, process it, and LEARN from it before going on. That takes strength and depth of character.

That can be you. That is you. Will you see yourself clearly? Will you admit your flaws honestly? Will you leverage your strengths joyfully and passionately? Will you have the strength of character to get back up and learn from it?

Mistakes happen. Defeats occur. Failure is inevitable. None of these are dirty words. Rather, they can be signs you're doing something tough, exciting, and out of the ordinary.

Choose to learn from the failure, and get back up.

3. Fear of failure stops forward movement

Fear is the many-faced god – it can take on different disguises. Fear can look like apathy. Fear can look like snarkiness. Fear can look like perfectionism. Fear can look like boredom. Fear can look like excuse-making. Fear can look like blame-shifting (blame, as Dr. Henry Cloud says, is the parking brake for improvement). Fear can be gazing in the rearview mirror living in the past. Fear can cause paralysis.

"The worst danger we face is the danger of being paralyzed by doubts and fears. The danger is brought on by those who abandon faith and sneer at hope. It is brought on by those who spread cynicism and distrust and try to blind us to the great chance to do good for all mankind."

~ President Harry S. Truman

Some may maintain the hope of forward momentum, but NEVER follow through. Procrastination robs you of your time, productivity, and full potential.

"There are risks and costs to a program of action, but they are far less than the long-range risks and costs of comfortable inaction."

~ President John F. Kennedy

In his book, *In Search of Excellence*, author Tom Peters underlines that there's nothing more inept than someone who ends his day and applauds himself, saying, *"Well, I made it through the day without screwing up."* The reality is, that's what many people do. Rather than pursuing well-meaning goals, they dodge the pain of making blunders and mistakes.

Be brave and move forward. Don't acquiesce to the voice of fear. You can forge ahead and still be afraid. Being afraid and bravery can coexist. I suppose some are naturally courageous and brave, seemingly carved out of heroic rock with an infrastructure of nerves of steel.

The reality is that if you have never known fear, then you have never had a requirement for courage. I'm very accustomed to fear, and courage has often demanded of me more than I have wanted.

Here's the deal: Courage is not a matter of birth. It is an expression of the heart.

"This idea that we're either courageous or chicken shit is just not true, because most of us are afraid and brave at the exact same moment, all day long."

~ Brené Brown

The reality is that you can't evade fear. No magic potion will remove fear. And, you can't wait for inspiration to accelerate you past the fear. Instead, to overcome fear, you have to feel the fear and take action anyway.

Will you allow yourself to sulk in self-pity and doubt, or rise to the occasion when you fail…and move forward? Be focused. Don't allow fear to allay forward movement. When paralysis wants to settle in – take action. *Action cures fear.* When the slug of procrastination knocks at your door, don't answer. Instead, move forward. That's how winning is done.

As our friend Rocky Balboa says:

Let me tell you something you already know. The world ain't all sunshine and rainbows. It's a very mean and nasty place, and I don't care how tough you are it will beat you to your knees and keep you there permanently if you let it. You, me, or nobody is gonna hit as hard as life. But it ain't about how hard ya hit. It's about how hard you get hit and keep moving forward. How much you can take and keep moving forward. That's how winning is done!

4. Stuck in a moment? Move past FEAR.

Have you ever felt stuck because of past failure? Are you stuck because of fear? Author Donald Miller says, "Fear is a manipulative emotion that can trick us into living a boring life."

What happens when we get stuck because of fear? We lose current and future opportunities for growth. We play it safe. We stop risking.

Larry Lauden, a contemporary philosopher of science, has spent years studying risk-management. His research suggests that fear (especially emerging from a past failure) causes leaders to suffer from *risk-lock*, a condition he likens to a gridlock, leaving us paralyzed, unable to do anything.

Can you think of a recent example where fear left you paralyzed from moving forward? Maybe it was learning a new skill or pursuing a challenging goal?

"We keep moving forward, opening new doors, and doing new things, because we're curious and curiosity keeps leading us down new paths."
~ Walt Disney

Let's be honest. If you step up to the plate, you are going to strike out sometimes. But the reality is, you have to step up to the plate.

Remaining stuck by past failure, or by fear, robs you from giving your peers, your team, your organization, and your customers your best.

Remember: Failure is not an event, it's a *judgment* about an event. Failure is the way we think about outcomes. Consider Jonas Salk, who created a vaccine for polio. Prior to creating the vaccine, he tried approximately two hundred times. Two hundred! Later someone asked him how it "felt to fail" two hundred times. His response was brilliant; he said:

I never failed two hundred times in my life. I was taught not to use the word "failure." I just discovered two hundred ways how not to vaccinate for polio.

What a great perspective, don't you think?

I recall hearing a story many years ago about Sir Edmund Hillary, a New Zealand mountaineer, who made several failed attempts at scaling Mount Everest before he finally achieved success. After one endeavor, he stood at the bottom of the giant mountain and shook his fist at it.

I'll defeat you yet, because you're as a big as you're going to get—but I'm still growing.

Every time Sir Edmund Hillary failed, he was also learning. Then, one day, he didn't fail.

Here's the reality: Failure is an *essential ingredient* to learning and growth. The failure that occurs in your life doesn't shape you, but how you *respond* to failure shapes you. (Read that sentence again... out loud!)

Really, the worst failure is not in the event itself. The worst failure is to choose to remain *paralyzed* by it. If we're not careful, we can stop moving forward and allow fear to have the upper hand.

Here is the deep truth about experiencing personal (leadership) growth: *The fear of stepping outside of your comfort zone will never go away.* Why? Because each time you venture into new terrain and embark on new challenges, you will experience fear.

One's own leadership journey is not a color-within-the-lines project—it's a work of art that requires you to move beyond your comfort zone. Leadership is about personal growth. Growth involves change. Change involves humility. Sometimes you need to bring about change. Sometimes you need to be changed.

Might I suggest that the limitations we are willing to accept establish the boundaries of your potential?

CALL TO ACTION

What is one step you can take to expand your comfort zone?

When you are paralyzed by fear, or stuck in a moment of past failure, you stop growing, you stop learning, you stop exploring, you stop discovering, and you stop dreaming. If you are stuck, stop looking backward, and dare to look forward. There are tremendous leadership moments that await you.

Fear seeks to establish limits to your personal leadership growth. Your leadership and life can be minimized or maximized in proportion to your courage.

Will you choose to be stuck in a moment of inaction, paralyzed by failure and fears? Or...instead, will you walk through the door of possibility with unbridled optimism, where rich opportunities grow and flourish?

HISTORY IS WAITING TO BE WRITTEN

"If you're going through hell, keep going."
~ Winston Churchill

Winston Churchill was once asked if he thought that history would speak kindly of him. His immediate response was, "History will be kind to me for I intend to write it." What a profound and courageous thing to proclaim, don't you think?

In 1940 Britain was on the edge of annihilation. Most of Europe had fallen. Hitler was about to launch "Operation Sea Lion" and defeat Britain.

The question the world asked was, "How will Britain survive?" Britain was walking the plank, doomed for destruction.

The BIG leadership lesson we can take from Winston Churchill is that his focus was not on survival. He said that his aim was to PREVAIL.

That shift in thinking is huge. Any time you find yourself grappling with the question, "How can I survive?" REJECT the question. Instead ask the question, "What does it mean to prevail in my situation? And then, how do I prevail?"

That is what England needed to hear. That is what they needed to be committed to. Surviving has the flavor of being a victim and reactive; prevailing has the notion of being proactive, tactical, and strategic.

Maybe you feel that you are in survival mode (taking on the position of defense). But...what if you put your focus on *prevailing*?

Imagine if Churchill had bowed to the edicts of others. More than likely history wouldn't have spoken so "kindly" of him. Maybe as leaders we can take a page out of Churchill's life and refuse to ask, "How will I survive" and instead ask, "How can I prevail?"

History stands at the doorway of our daily lives waiting to etch a story … our story. We don't have to be the victims of past mistakes and failures. Allow past mistakes and failures to be stepping stones rather than stumbling blocks.

Will history be kind to you? It most certainly can be.

The fertile ground of tomorrow waits for YOU to scribe the epic story you were intended to live.

CALL TO ACTION

Identify where you are living in survival mode. Here are some simple actionable steps:

- Write on a 3x5 card 1 or 2 ways you can shift your thinking.
- Create an action plan.
- Identify 2 or 3 mentors who are further along professionally.
- Enhance your skillset through training.

History will be kind, for YOU will write it.

GET IN THE GAME

"It is not the critic who counts: not the man who points out how the strong man stumbles or where the doer of deeds could have done better. The credit belongs to the man who is actually in the arena, whose face is marred by dust and sweat and blood, who strives valiantly, who errs and comes up short again and again, because there is no effort without error or shortcoming, but who knows the great enthusiasms, the great devotions, who spends himself for a worthy cause; who, at the best, knows, in the end, the triumph of high achievement, and who, at the worst, if he fails, at least he fails while daring

greatly, so that his place shall never be with those cold and timid souls who knew neither victory nor defeat."
~ Theodore Roosevelt

Being brave requires you to get in the game. As a player in any sport, or in life for that matter, requires you to enter the arena…to get in the game. Now, in the finals of any sport, we see the best of the best enter the arena, where a champ will emerge. As a player, one yearns to be in the game, to be part of something great. Players put on their jerseys with hopes of contributing to the game, maybe even making the game-winning play.

A game, at its heart, is the creation of a challenge to test oneself. The ancient Greeks saw games as opportunities to foster that excellence of spirit, mind, and body that they called *arete*—something that could extend to overcoming challenges in every area of life.

Imagine that you are being asked to take part in the BIG game. The gauntlet has been thrown down. The competition is tough. Strategies are being carefully crafted. As a player on the team, will you choose to stay on the sidelines and be a spectator, or will you be a playmaker?

We are designed to be IN the game; our heart is saying "Put me in the game!"

You were *not* designed to sit on the bench.

Here are some simple things to consider:

1. Competition enhances your game

The triumph of winning is important, but just entering the arena tests an individual's personal leadership. The game of business competition enhances one's skills. What makes a game a game is that it poses a problem, a particular challenge to overcome.

Opponents push us to new levels of effort and leadership excellence. The real challenge is to extend your best and to see if you can persevere without quitting in the face of demand.

Drive, grit, and the will to win. We are deeply moved by the display of competitive greatness. Because it's in the challenge that we're tested and our *best* is required.

2. The game is not over

The reality is that all of us have made mistakes and failed.

If we're not careful, it can be easy to *live* in the arena of past defeats and failures. Staying in the space of unproductive self-talk infringes on our ability to see and experience future success.

In 1929, Roy Riegels made UCLA history. It was in the Rose Bowl against Georgia Tech. Georgia Tech fumbled the ball. Riegels played for UCLA. He picked up the ball and got confused. He began to run in the wrong direction. Sixty-five yards in the wrong direction. Finally, a member of his own team tackled him.

Think about that for a minute. That's embarrassing. The team was devastated. They finally got to half-time and went to their locker room. They felt beat up!

Can you relate? Do you ever feel like in your own journey that you fumbled the ball or, worse, that you picked up the ball and ran it in the wrong direction? Maybe for years or maybe for decades? Now you want a fresh start.

That's how Riegels felt. He was beat up. Usually, when coaches are in the locker room between halves, they are pretty animated, aren't they? They have quite a few things to say. However, when Coach Nibs Price went into the locker room, he sat in silence for the entire halftime. Finally, the timekeeper came in and said, "Coach, it's time." He looked up at his team and said, "The same men who started the first half will start the second half."

Everybody began to file out, everybody but Riegels. The coach walked over to Riegels, put his arm around him and said, "Did you hear me, son? The game is not over yet."

Some of you might have failed, think that you've blown it. You've made mistakes. You have feelings of inadequacy and tremendous guilt. The good news is that the game is *not* over yet. You're still alive. The sun came up again. The game is not over.

3. Put on your jersey

Maybe you had a dream or something you wanted to do, but people around you told you that you were too fat, too thin, too tall, too short, too smart, too dumb, too this or too that…to accomplish whatever it is you want to accomplish. Have you ever been there?
I find that the place of most resistance can be the place of greatest opportunity.

Don't *wait* for others to rise above mediocrity. Set the tone yourself. Rise above the challenges, avoid the pitfall of self-pity and dig your heels into the dirt with unyielding determination and grit. Stand tall above the obstacles around you. I promise, it's possible. When you do, it will surprise you.

Game day (today) is not the time to:

- Leave the arena with an unmarred and clean jersey.
- Decide you'll win when things get easier.
- Exhibit subpar performance.
- Blame-shift, whine, or play the victim.

The scope of your untapped human potential is a gift to the team players around you. The only one forcing you to replay the game of worry, self-doubt, and fear is YOU.

What if you truly believed that? What would your day look like if you chose to dig deep and put on your jersey? What would it look like if you walked through your day with confidence instead of frustration and indifference? The choice is YOURS.

The voice of uncertainty, mediocrity, past failures, and naysayers are silenced—as we step into the arena with gusto, recognizing that this season of leadership has profound possibilities.

Your family, your business, your team and your customers want your best!

Get in the game…fully.

LOOKING THROUGH NEW LENS

When my oldest son was 3 years old, he put a pair of sunglasses on and said, with surprise in his voice, "Daddy, I have a new pair of eyes!" Well, son, not exactly. Then again, maybe he's on to something.

How would your life and leadership look with a new pair of eyes, or by looking through a new set of lenses? With a new pair of lenses, what incredible opportunities might you see? How might you be brave in new ways and maximize the possibilities in front of you?

Rosamund Stone Zander, who wrote the book, *The Art of Possibility*, conveys a powerful story to help further illustrate this point:

> *A shoe factory sends two marketing scouts to a region of Africa to study the prospects for expanding business. One sends back a telegram saying, "SITUATION HOPELESS. NO ONE WEARS SHOES."*
> *The other writes back triumphantly, "GLORIOUS BUSINESS OPPORTUNITY. THEY HAVE NO SHOES."*

To the marketing expert who sees no shoes, all the evidence points to hopelessness. To his colleague, the same conditions point to abundance and possibility.

What's interesting is that both individuals are in the same environment, circumstances, time, and place, yet they have a different pair of "lenses" through which they see the situation.

What are the blinders holding us back from recognizing and seeing through the *lens of abundance and possibility*? Is our belief system causing us to peer through tainted lenses, prohibiting us from seeing the opportunities in front of us?

The lens of "believing it is possible"

> *"Believe and act as if it were impossible to fail."*
> ~ Charles F. Kettering

Belief governs what we achieve in life. We're constantly storing up things in our inner life: *good, bad, true, or false*. What enters your mind occupies it. It is then expressed in what you do, what you say, in your character, and your life.

Think about how your brain is wired. Your brain is designed to solve any problem and reach any goal that you give it. Belief in great outcomes is the prevailing force, the power behind all great art, books, plays, technological advances, and scientific discoveries. Disbelief, on the other hand, is a negative power. A mind filled with doubt begins to encourage reasons for disbelief. Think doubt and miss the mark. Think victory and thrive.

Fear may be causing you to shrink back. Fear stops people from capitalizing on the possible. Fear can be a powerful voice that prohibits you from seeing through the lens of possibility. Here's a simple cure to fear. Write this down. *Action cures fear.*

If you are going to be successful, you need to give up the phrase "I can't" and all of its friends, such as "I wish I were able to," "it won't work," and "no use trying." Those words dis-empower you. The words you think and say actually affect your body and your outcome.

Even those you surround yourself with will impact whether you see something as possible, or impossible. Who are you spending the most time with these days? When you surround yourself with great people, it makes you better. If you want to live a life of adventure and possibility, then choose a tribe of people who make life an adventure and see the world through the lens of possibilities.

When our lives are filled with expectation and possibility, we are guided by faith and driven by hope to do *nothing* less than create a bright future.

The lens of "believing in yourself"

"There is no passion to be found playing small – in settling for a life that is less than the one you are capable of living."
~ Nelson Mandela

You have what it takes. You have significance. You have purpose. You have a destiny. You matter. You have the right stuff to make it happen. You have to believe you have the right stuff. You have to believe in yourself. Believing in yourself is a choice. You must choose to believe that you can do anything you set your mind to, anything at all!

It's your personal responsibility to take control of your self-concept and your beliefs. If you assume in favor of yourself and act as if it is possible, then you will do the things that are necessary to bring about the results. If you believe it is impossible, you will *not* focus on what is necessary, and you will not yield the results. It develops into a self-fulfilling prophecy.

Today we are being invited into the world of abundance and possibility, by looking through new lenses to see the extraordinary opportunities in front of us.

Are you wearing the right lenses?

Power of OTHERS

Chapter 5
Power of Others

During one visit to NYC, we were able to visit one of the many companies the Billionaire owned. One of his executives was giving us a tour and explaining some of the processes that went into putting together their products and services. It was both amazing and exhilarating!

What I remember vividly is that while we walked around this organization, the Billionaire would comment on the different employees' work with kind and encouraging words...suggesting that their work was important, that it made a difference to the organization. Even in the small gestures and comments, you could see the employees' eyes light up. As the old adage goes, "a long time after people forgot what you have said, they will remember how you made them feel."

You may never realize how your positive feedback, or lack thereof, will lift or deflate the people around you. The emotional equity you build with people, by focusing on what they do well is critical—it's irreplaceable. Point out to them how they contribute to the organization. Show kindness. People want to know they matter.

BELIEVING IN OTHERS:
GIVING SOMETHING MORE THAN A PAYCHECK

"Treat a man as he appears to be and you make him worse. But treat a man as if he already were what he potentially could be, and you make him what she should be."
~ Johann Wolfgang Von Goethe

People are your prize. People are your treasure. It pays rich dividends to believe in others. Believing the best in people usually brings the best out in people.

Every day you are provided an extraordinary opportunity to breathe life into someone with your words and actions. Encouragement and appreciation are oxygen for the soul. How are you igniting life and confidence into those around you? Do your teams, coworkers, and others know that you are *for* them?

Infuse value in others

"You need to be aware of what others are doing, applaud their efforts, acknowledge their successes, and encourage them in their pursuits. When we all help one another, everybody wins."
~ Jim Stovall

Somebody said recently that what the world needs is not more geniuses but more *genius makers*, people who enhance and don't diminish the gift of those around them. Believe that *others* have what it takes.

We are either making deposits into someone's life or making withdrawals. A basic truth is that people will always move toward anyone who increases them and away from others who diminish them. You can enrich others by pointing out their strengths, and partner to work on development opportunities.

Encourage others

"There comes that mysterious meeting in life when someone acknowledges who we are and what we can be, igniting the circuits of our highest potential."
~ Rusty Berkus

Look for the gold in others. Maybe it's encouraging others to chart new territory, challenging them to break free from the status quo. Be aggressive about recognizing the best in people and look to develop their strengths. I dare you to leave behind the easy route of highlighting just someone's shortcomings and failures.

Richard Branson, founder of Virgin Mobile, says, *"You shouldn't be looking for people slipping up, you should be looking for all the good things people do and praising those."*

Lift others up

"We rise by lifting others."
~ Robert Ingersoll

Many people have few, if any, people who believe in them, who lift them up. Most people know when someone believes in them. Many leaders spend time trying to get others to think highly of them, when instead they should try to get their people to think highly of themselves. When a person has no one in their corner cheering them on, they are likely to struggle with feelings of loneliness and discouragement.

"I have never seen a man who could do real work except under the stimulus of encouragement and enthusiasm, and the approval of the people for whom he is working."
~ Charles Schwab

Here, drawn from a story by author and technology investor Barry Libert, is a story that encapsulates beautifully the power of believing in others:

> *[Retired United States Navy] Captain Mike Abrashoff knows the importance of saying 'thank you.' In his first book, It's Your Ship, he related how he sent letters to the parents of his crew members on the guided-missile destroyer USS Benfold. Putting himself in those parents' shoes, he imagined how happy they would be to hear from the commanding officer that their sons and daughters were doing well. And he figured that those parents would, in turn, call their children to tell them how proud they were of them.*
>
> *Abrashoff debated whether to send a letter to the parents of one young man who wasn't really star material. Weighing the sailor's progress, he decided to go ahead. A couple of weeks later, the sailor appeared at his door, tears streaming down his face. It seems the kid's father had always considered him a failure and told him so. After reading the captain's letter, he called to congratulate his son and tell him how proud he was of him. 'Captain, I can't thank you enough,' said the young man. For the first time in his life, he felt loved and encouraged by his father.*

Captain Mike Abrashoff says, *"Leadership is the art of practicing simple things—commonsense gestures that ensure high morale and vastly increase the odds of winning."*

Every day we are presented with the opportunity to believe in others, and make deposits into a person's emotional bank account through our words and actions.

CALL TO ACTION

Take time this week to infuse value in others, encourage others, and lift others up. What if…what if…the act of believing in others was part of the trajectory, the catalyst even, to fuel others to live the best version of themselves? How are you going to deliver more than a paycheck, and believe in others today?

THE POWER OF HOPE

One of my favorite movies is *The Shawshank Redemption*. A tale of hope in the midst of despair, of redemption on the other side of suffering, it tells the story of Andy Dufresne (played by Tim Robbins), a successful banker condemned to Shawshank prison for the murder of his wife and her lover.

In the movie, the two central characters, Andy Dufresne and Red (played by Morgan Freeman), have a running dialogue about hope.

Red warns Andy that "hope can be a dangerous thing"…which we soon discover is the entire point of *The Shawshank Redemption*— that fear can hold you prisoner and *hope* can set you free. To Andy, to quit hoping is to start dying.

Hope is a powerful element, which can breathe life into others. Although not a strategy, there's a power in HOPE that goes beyond explanation. It lifts us out of the debris of our failures, our pain, and our fears.

We are people of hope. We were made to be people of hope. We are made to infuse others with hope.

Each attempt to succeed, each moment we are driven to pursue a dream, advance a cause, encourage those around you, or work to make the world better, is an act of HOPE.

I remember as a kid, during Thanksgiving, my sister and I would grab the ends of the wishbone from the turkey and break it with a *hope* that a wish would come true. My son recently celebrated his birthday, and we asked him to make a wish, with the hope that by blowing out the candles that wish would somehow come true. We love to hope.

You were DESIGNED for hope

"Hope propels you during difficult times and infuses you with happiness and

keeps you moving towards your dreams, goals and aspirations... So what is hope?
Healthy—Optimism—People—Enable."
~ Glenn Llopis

YOU were designed for HOPE. It's as though your soul cannot live deprived of a belief in the future. Consider your body, which needs water to survive—so your soul needs hope to flourish and prevail.

What innovative solutions have you given up on at work? Are you allowing the nagging voice of fear to choke out the hope of a bright tomorrow? How might you be allowing hope to remain dormant inside you?

You were designed for hope.

I heard someone say years ago that the richest place on the planet is not the diamond mines of South Africa or the oil fields of Kuwait. The richest place on the planet is the cemetery. In the cemetery, we bury inventions never produced; ideas and dreams that never became reality; and hopes and aspirations that were never pursued.

Who will you allow to dictate what is to be deemed as possible in your life and leadership? The flags of all your tomorrows have sailed at half-mast. It is time to raise them once again! You were designed for hope.

Hope cannot be DELEGATED

"Leaders instill in their people a hope for success and a belief in themselves.
Positive leaders empower people to accomplish their goals."
~ Unknown

As a leader, one thing you cannot do is delegate hope. Do you lead a team, a department, organization, or project? Hope must be a part of your makeup. A part of your leadership tool chest. A leader can always delegate tasks, assignments, initiatives, but *not* hope.

Stop for a moment (no, seriously...stop)...and think about a leader who brought "hope" to a situation. What did it look like? What did it feel like?

Can you imagine being in the middle of the Great Depression, and what it would have been like to lead a nation that was at the tipping point of implosion? It was said that during the days of the Great Depression, President Franklin D. Roosevelt had the aptitude to convey hope and confidence; to allow others to walk away feeling more cheerful, stronger in themselves and what they were to accomplish, and determined to see things through despite tough times.

Be a DEALER in hope

> *"A leader is a dealer in hope."*
> ~ Napoleon Bonaparte

What a thought.

Leaders can help breathe oxygen into the soul. They can kick-start a demoralized team into action.

Consider the words of Martin Luther King Jr., who procured hope through his life and the "I have a dream" speech. Luther suggested that it was possible for a desired future where blacks, whites, and others could coexist together harmoniously as equals. He was a dealer in hope.

Winston Churchill gave hope to England when hope seemed inconceivable. While leaders and diplomats of his country were trying to figure out how to "survive," Churchill took a different path, inspiring hope by helping the country see that they could "prevail." He was a dealer in hope.

On the other hand, a leader who is a dealer in hope will be charging forward and determined to see and call the best out of others. When individuals see a leader with unbridled (not blind) optimism who radiates a sense that collectively, as a team, we can do what needs to be done, then people don't waste their energy wondering "if" but focus their energy going after "how" (not problem-minded, but solution-minded).

Remember, as leaders (whether in title or not) you:

... were designed for hope

... cannot delegate hope

... and are a dealer in hope!

Our desire to endure and preserve is fueled by this one seemingly innocuous element called HOPE.

THE POWER OF APPRECIATION

"Appreciation is a wonderful thing. It makes what is excellent in others belong to us as well."
~ Voltaire

Have you ever observed one of those inspiring moments where you saw a level of gratitude, appreciation, and generosity offered to someone else? Well, I had one of those moments recently.

I walked into a gas station to get a soft drink, and as I was checking out there were two gentlemen in line in front of me. The first was a young man dressed in his military uniform, and the second an older gentleman. The older gentleman leaned in quickly while the military man was checking out, and told the lady behind the counter, "Whatever this man wants is on me." The older gentleman turned to the man dressed in uniform and said, "Thank you…thank you for what you represent and what you've committed to on behalf of the United States. Thank you for serving us and loving us enough to wear that uniform. We are SO grateful. Thank you."

(A brief pause, which felt like an eternity, but it was so touching that you didn't want to rush the moment with words.)

The older gentleman then looked at the lady behind the counter, who now had tears flowing down her cheek. "Ma'am, I want you to give this man whatever he wants." "Sir," now speaking to the young service man, "I see you're buying gas; that's on me. I see you're buying food; that's on me. Please...please, put more on the counter. It's the least I can do."

By this time tears were welling up in my eyes, as I felt this great sense of pride and appreciation for both the man who was serving our country, and also for the gentleman who took the time and used his resources to exhibit his appreciation. In many ways, this older gentleman showed tremendous servant leadership.

I wondered to myself, as I walked out of the gas station, how many times we miss moments like this...where we could extend a hand of gratitude by offering an encouraging word, a thank you, and/or a gesture of generosity.

CALL TO ACTION

This week, join me in being a first class "appreciator." How might you show appreciation to someone this week? Choose 1 or 2 people this week that you are going to show appreciation to.

Each of us has an extraordinary opportunity to set the tone for the people we want to be, and inspire others to what they could become. Each of us has been gifted with *talent, treasure, and time* that we could graciously extend to others.

It could be that we are paralyzed, if you will, waiting for something big to give ourselves to. However, what if in the waiting for the big "spectacular" we are missing the everyday ordinary moments to be extraordinary in the seemingly mundane and boring. Start by simply saying "thank you."

Let's move beyond being just an *observer* to being an active *participant,* and extend a hand of generosity and gratitude for someone else that could use recognition. A simple thank you and a show of appreciation can make all the difference.

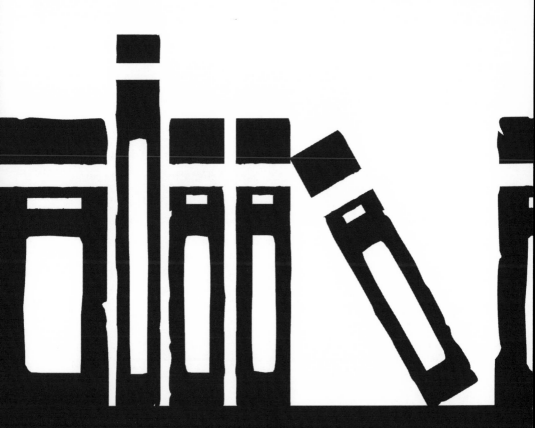

Contentment
is a learned behavior

Chapter 6
Lure of Approval

One night during a pre-dinner conversation, someone in our group was upset about the criticism from a business partner. I remember the Billionaire, again chuckling, dismissing the critical words and suggesting that if we were to try and please everyone in business, we would get nowhere.

As leaders, there are times you can feel like you are on an island. Sometimes you have to make tough calls, unpopular decisions, or lead in uncertain times. If we were to try and please everyone whom we are leading, we will ultimately become ineffective. The Pulitzer Prize-winning journalist, Herbert Swope, said:

"I can't give you a surefire formula for success, but I can give you a formula for failure: try to please everybody all the time."

THE APPROVAL MONSTER

"Our deepest fear is not that we are inadequate. Our deepest fear is that we are powerful beyond measure. It is our light, not our darkness, that most frightens us. We ask ourselves, Who am I to be brilliant, gorgeous, talented, fabulous? Actually, who are you not to be? You are a child of God. Your

playing small does not serve the world. There is nothing enlightened about shrinking so that other people won't feel insecure around you. We are all meant to shine, as children do. We were born to make manifest the glory of God that is within us. It's not just in some of us; it's in everyone. And as we let our own light shine, we unconsciously give other people permission to do the same. As we are liberated from our own fear, our presence automatically liberates others."

~ Marianne Williamson

Some people live in bondage to what others think of them—getting easily hurt by another's words, habitually comparing themselves to other people, creating competition in the most ordinary situations. This person has fallen prey to the approval monster.

"Comparison is the thief of joy."
~ Theodore Roosevelt

Sometimes, because of this need for approval, we can put on this façade, this mask—pretending to be someone we are not.

We become good at impression management. Impression management is when we try to steer others opinions of us by pretending to be what others think will be acceptable.

The propensity to hide who we really are and be something we are not is so alluring that psychologists occasionally refer to this as the *imposter phenomenon*. It's this general sense that at some level I'm pretending; if others knew the truth about me, the dance would be over. I would be finished.

So we spin the truth. Instead of living our authentic selves, we become pros at impression management. We enter this amateur-like life in the service of impressing others.

If we're honest with ourselves, at times, like other addicts, we will strive in unhealthy ways to get a fix when we feel anxious or desperate. Perhaps, like other addicts, we discover that no fix endures or lasts forever. Yet, we find ourselves coming back for more. In this situation, we are dealing with an approval monster.

At times, the approval monster takes the shape of perfectionism. As the beloved sociologist Brené Brown has shared, if perfectionism is driving you, then shame is riding shotgun. Brené suggests that, "We struggle with perfectionism in areas where we feel most vulnerable to shame."

Perfectionism, then, is a way of thinking that says that "If we look perfect, live perfectly, work perfectly, and act perfectly, we can avoid or minimize criticism, blame, judgment, shame, and ridicule."

Here's the deal. Perfectionism is not about striving for excellence. It's not about growth, development, and achievement. Somewhere along the way, we embraced this draining (false) belief system: *I am what I accomplish and how well I accomplish it.*

This reel goes on in our heads, at times, "Please. Perform. Perfectly."

I like to call this perfectionism, *The Trinity of False Identity:*

- I am what I do.
- I am how well I do it.
- I am how much I do.

Here's what Brené Brown suggests is the difference between Healthy Striving and Perfectionism:

> *Healthy striving, meanwhile, focuses on you. It occurs when you ask yourself, "How can I improve?" Perfectionism keeps the focus on others. It occurs when you ask, "What will they think?" Research, unfortunately, shows that perfectionism hampers success and often leads to depression, anxiety, addiction and missed opportunities, due to fears of putting anything out in the world that could be imperfect or disappoint others. It's a 20-ton shield that we lug around thinking it will protect us when, in fact, it's the thing that's really preventing us from taking flight. Another way to think about it? Consider Leonard Cohen's song "Anthem," which says, "There's a crack in everything. That's how the light gets in."*

The substitute to this addiction

"One of the fine arts of gracious living is the art of living freely with our critics. When we have the grace to be free in the presence of those who judge our lives and evaluate our actions, we have freedom."
~ Lewis Smedes

What if we decided that criticism would no longer rock our boat? That our life's balance and sense of well-being wasn't resting on acceptance from others?

Imagine in situations where someone expresses disapproval of you, and instead of being bent toward gaining their approval, you instead felt genuine love toward them. Imagine being freed from the unhealthy need to astound and impress those around you. Imagine your sense of self was no longer leaning on the unstable foundation of whether somebody notices how attractive, smart, or successful you are. Imagine with me for a moment. It IS possible.

Let's be honest. We all know what that drug tastes like. To strive for others' approval and how it feels when it gets withheld.

This problem is almost like a mental jury box composed of all the people who rate us like so many judges, calculating our every move and assessing us. That jury box can certainly get overcrowded. Parents are in that box. I imagine some school teachers are there, too, and some important members of our peer group, and don't forget our boss, co-workers, family members, and neighbors.

When our identity is wrapped up in whether we are perceived as successful, we are set up to be trapped by the approval monster. Our sense of self is on the line.

"Who am I?" Henri Nouwen asks. "I am the one who is liked, praised, admired, disliked, hated, or despised. Whether I am a pianist, a businessman, or a minister, what matters is how I am perceived by my world. If being busy is important to others, then I must be busy.

If having money is a sign of real freedom, then I must claim my money. If knowing many people proves my importance, I will have to make the necessary contacts."

Maybe this monster-like figure takes form when you *find yourself OFTEN* getting hurt by what others say about you…and the noise starts…

Maybe you find yourself *habitually comparing* yourself to other people…and the noise continues…

Maybe you have a nagging sense that you aren't important enough or special enough…

Maybe the ugly monster *is you trying to impress important people….*

Eventually, the noise gets so loud and the monster so overpowering that you just want it to STOP.

Here's an important reality. If you don't remember anything else, remember this…YOU are not the passive victim of others' sentiments, thoughts, and feelings about you. Their views are feeble and powerless until you endorse them. Their opinions have no weight until you validate them. No one's approval will impact your life unless you *allow* it importance and prominence.

It's your choice.

Pulling yourself out of approval addiction

Brené Brown has an incredible exercise and visual reminder for pulling yourself out of the approval addiction spiral.

1. Cut out a 1-inch square of paper.
2. Write down the names of the people whose opinions matter the most to you. Remember, you can only write as many words that can fit on that piece of paper.
3. Refer to it whenever you start to feel yourself spiraling.

I'm confident this exercise will not only help you reset your thinking, but it will also be equally inspiring. How many times have you been in the middle of working on a big project only to see that someone else is doing something similar? Or how often do you stop dead in your tracks, giving up before you've really even started, because of a critical comment someone made about your process?

This exercise is intended to remind us of the people who actually matter in our life. When you feel the need to seek approval, seek it from them, from the people who love you enough to be tough when necessary, but not for sport.

The delusion and entrapment of more

I think one of the most challenging places that approval monster likes to fester and rear its ugly head is the entrapment of MORE.

Don't we all get entangled with the enemy of "more"…more money, more clothes, more shoes, more stuff…more kids (okay, maybe not more kids, :) although we have four boys). I digress.

We believe that MORE will get us approval from others or help us approve of ourselves. But is MORE ever enough?

We kill ourselves for more—*more stuff, more achievements, more experiences, more successes, and more choices.* We're showered, every day, by thousands of messages that convey that more, eventually, will lead to contentment.

The truth is there is something called *learned contentment.* Contentment is a learned behavior, and it depends on the perspective you bring to life. It's not something you find; it's an attitude you bring to life.

There is a Peanuts cartoon where Snoopy was sitting on top of his doghouse on Thanksgiving. He's bitter because Charlie Brown and the family are having this huge feast inside their house, and Snoopy is stuck on his doghouse with only dog food. He's grumbling about this until a thought occurs to him and he says to himself, *"I guess it could be worse. I could have been born a turkey."*

Prayer and solitude

Carving out times for prayer and solitude helps us to see what is important in life. It helps us peel away the noise of distraction and the vices of our culture. Among other things, it allows us to remember what's important in our life.

Maybe you've been choked by this constant need for others' approval. Rather than experiencing a sense of calm, peace and joy, you find yourself:

- Feeling angry and yelling at children too often.
- Feeling envious of people more successful or attractive than you.
- Passing judgment on people.
- Worrying too much about your money and job.
- Spinning the truth in order to gain others approval.

Many spiritual practices over the centuries have shown the powerful benefits of carving out time for silence, prayer, meditation, and solitude. In fact, prayer and solitude can become the furnace of transformation, burning off the need for self-importance, validation from others' opinions, self-centeredness, and so much more.

What makes prayer and solitude so important? It's one place where we can discover freedom from the forces of an external world that can sometimes ruthlessly mold us.

In his book, *Tools of Titans*, Tim Ferriss sat down with more than 200 executives, leaders, and other people at the heights of their fields, where he found that 80% had some form of guided meditation, prayer, or mindfulness practice. (A great tool to start mediation is the app headspace, found at www.headspace.com).

As with solitude, as the heart of the matter, it is primarily about NOT doing something. Just as the spiritual practice of fasting means to abstain from eating, so solitude means to abstain from society. When we go into solitude, we remove ourselves from others, from conversation, from noise, from the constant onslaught of activities.

"In solitude," Henri Nouwen wrote, "I get rid of my scaffolding."

Scaffolding is all the immaterial items we use to prop ourselves up, to assure ourselves that we are so significant or acceptable. In solitude and quiet, neither achievements nor résumés nor assets nor networks define us.

One of the biggest distractions in our culture is TV. Maybe just *for a week* you decide to limit the amounts of TV you watch…just to set aside moments of meditation and solitude.

Maybe you decide to cut TV COLD TURKEY! Maybe you say, "all right."

For one week, I am not going to watch a single thing on TV, except whenever the Dallas Cowboys play. Other than that, it's not going to happen.

I can't remember the last time that I talked to someone who said, "Last night I spent the whole night watching TV, and today I'm filled with so much love and peace and joy."

When I find myself comparing myself to others (remember, "comparison is the thief of joy") or thinking, "I could be happy if I had their stuff, their job, or their life"…I then realize that I need to step away and listen for another voice that isn't thirsting for human recognition.

Maybe the voice says something like, "Do not look down on your place, your gifts, or your voice…"

Because…YOU are worth it

The Approval Monster would have you to believe you are not worth something at the present, but imagine if I were handing you a $100 bill. Would you take it? I'm sure you would. But first, let me illustrate an invaluable principle.

I am going to crumple the bill up. Do you still want it? I'm sure you do!

Well, next I take that $100 and drop it on the ground and begin to grind it into the floor with my shoe. Now with it all crumpled and dirty, I hold it out to you. Do you still want it? I'm suspecting that you do!

No matter what I did to the money, you still wanted it because it did not decrease in value. It was still worth $100.

Here's the beautiful reality. Many times in our lives, we are dropped, crumpled, and ground into the dirt by the decisions we make and the circumstances that come our way. We feel as though we are worthless. But no matter what has happened or what will happen, we will never lose our value, especially in the eyes of the Divine. Dirty or clean, crumpled or finely creased, we are still priceless to Him.

In the ancient text etched by the apostle Paul, these inspiring words were written, "YOU are God's masterpiece." Our desire for approval can truly be met by receiving God's acceptance and approval of us.

No spare parts

I believe your life is a gift. You are on purpose. You have divine significance. You matter in life.

Years ago, when my first son, George, was born, we purchased a dresser from IKEA for his clothes. When we got it home and opened up the box – we spread the various parts all over the floor. There were screws, bolts, nails, plugs, wood, and more! I quickly realized that I was in way over my head. Reading through the directions and reviewing the diagrams, I noticed at the top were the three worst words ever written in the existence of man: SOME ASSEMBLY REQUIRED.

Those three words strike fear into dads all around the world—even to this day.

As I finished putting the cabinet together, I found that I had several pieces left (three screws, four nails, three washers, and an acrylic piece that said "important" on it). I had a bunch of spare parts left over!

Here's the deal.

There was a voice in my soul, in that moment, whispering oh so gently, as I stared at the many spare parts. (May you not forget this truth.) The still small voice said, "YOU are not a spare part. The people you come in contact with every day are not spare parts. You have a purpose. You have a destiny."

May you never forget that you are on purpose. You have significance. You matter. You are not a spare part.

Optimizing your Energy

Chapter 7
Optimizing Your Energy

The last few years of the Billionaire's life, with the myriad stories I heard and many things I observed, one thing held true: He was adamant about the importance of using one's time wisely on this earth. (Keep in mind, he was in his early to mid-80s when he was doling out this advice.) How will you serve others, what type of legacy will you choose to lead, what type of relationships will you build, etc.?

To maximize the time you have, be intentional about where you put your time and energy. He was resolute that your energy is your most precious commodity. The question is, where will you place your energy?

HABITS, ROUTINES, AND OPTIMIZING SIMPLICITY

"If you want to change your life you have to change something you do every day."
~ John Maxwell

One of the things I've lamented is how much of my life I've wasted living a life of obligation rather than a life of intention. If you don't plan your day, someone will plan it for you. Let me take it a step further...if you don't write your life script, someone will write it for you. You will either choose your life, or you will live a life that is chosen and defined by others.

Change your routines, change your life

People who manage to get a lot accomplished each day aren't super-human; they've just grasped and implemented a few simple routines and habits. There is a lot of research that would suggest that the greatest performers have the greatest routines. What makes genius is less about genetics and more about routines and habits.

Having routines and rituals in your life provides a steady framework in which creative advances often transpire. They open up time and space for recovery and renewal. The sustaining power of routines and rituals comes from the reality that they protect and preserve their energy.

We must add routines to our (personal and professional) life, which reduces the amount of (limited) determination necessary in order to preserve a state of uninterrupted attention.

As journalist Mason Currey, who researched and catalogued over many years the routines and habits of famous writers, thinkers, and creatives said:

> *There is a popular notion that artists work from inspiration—that there is some strike or bolt or bubbling up of creative mojo from who knows where... but I hope [my work] makes clear that waiting for inspiration to strike is a terrible, terrible plan. In fact, perhaps the single best piece of advice I can offer to anyone trying to do creative work is to ignore inspiration.*

I read recently that David Brooks, in a *New York Times* column on the topic of crafting systems, habits and routines, summarized this more candidly: "[Great minds] think like artists but work like accountants."

Be your best, eliminate the rest

Data and thought leaders of our day would say that the high-performers of our day go a step further. They let go of things that *are working* if they are NOT the *best things*. What that simply means is that they are able to let go of things that take up a lot of energy, time, and resources that may be good, and even profitable, but are keeping them from the best things. Even good things can be the enemy of the best things.

The reality is that you probably won't let go of old things and embrace the new, best things if you stay attached to what has been hijacking your energy. Consider a child who has to get rid of the tricycle if he wants to ride a two-wheeler. Consider the snake that sheds its skin to make room for the new one. You can't have both, the old and new, because beneath the old is a bright and glistening new, ready, and waiting.

I'm reminded of the story of Steve Jobs, after coming back as CEO of Apple. During his time away, Microsoft had taken over the world. Apple barely had a pulse. But Steve Jobs comes back. He finds out that Apple had manufactured dozens of different Macintosh desktops, laptops, and servers in a dizzying collection of variations, as well as many other ancillary items, few of which made a profit.

He keeps asking the same question over and over again, "if I want to have my nephew buy something, which one does he buy?"

Ultimately, Jobs axed more than 70 percent of Apple's hardware and software products. Jobs wiped the slate clean.

Jobs brings all his senior leaders into a room after assessing the landscape of Apple. He goes up to a big white board and draws a two-by-two matrix. Four quadrants. Across the top, he writes personal / professional, and across the side he writes desktop / portable. He proclaims that "if it doesn't fit into these quadrants, then we are going to cut it out."

Focus on what you are going to be the best at, and eliminate the rest.

Produce high-quality work

Prolific writer Adam Grant uses the following equation that drives a law of productivity.

$$High\text{-}Quality\ Work\ Produced =$$
$$(Time\ Spent) \times (Intensity\ of\ Focus)$$

In essence, he groups his work into a focused and uninterrupted rhythm; where he maximizes his concentration and intensity when he works, and he capitalizes on the results he produces per unit of time spent working. The type of work generating the results you want in your life requires enhancing your performance by relentless focused work.

As an aside, doing less shouldn't be translated as being lazy. Don't give in to a cultural pitfall that values personal sacrifice over personal productivity.

There's a big difference between being productive and being busy. Instead of measuring the quantity of work you do, measure results in terms of the amount of time that yields the greatest return.

Eliminate work for work's sake.

The deception of multitasking

You can't multitask.

We believe we can multitask. The most common ways that we multitask:

- Watching a football game while your kids are trying to talk with you
- Meeting with colleagues while responding to emails
- Being on a date with your significant other and checking social media on your phone

You can't multitask. Let me say it, again. You cannot multitask.

Neuroscience shows us that you're incapable of multitasking.

Multitasking means you're doing more than one thing, and you're not. What you're doing are one or two things with less efficiency than if you were doing one thing at a time.

I'm not busy; it's just not a priority

Busy isn't busy. Busy is a lack of priority. We can become addicted to busy.

Busy is a DECISION. If you want to do something really badly, you MAKE the time.

If you are saying you are too busy, see where your time is being allocated. Are you too busy watching Netflix and binge-watching shows? Are you spending too much time puttering around with frivolous stuff?

Busyness many times is a proxy for productivity. Without clear criteria or indicators of what it means to be productive, we associate busyness with productivity. In other words, doing lots of stuff in a visible manner.

Say "no" to many small things to say "yes" to a few big things. The barrier to a meaningful life is not a lack of commitment, but over-commitment. Just because you're busy doesn't mean you're doing the *right* things. Just because you can do something does not mean you *should* do something. Conversely, you also need to not do the things everyone else is doing. Do the things that give you the highest return on investment of your time and energy.

Energy is especially important to manage well. Your energy is indiscriminate; it will be allocated wherever you put it. The reality is that energy is a finite resource that is rarely managed well.

Some would say that your energy is your most precious commodity. Regardless of who you are, you have only a finite amount of it. In reality, managing energy, not time, is the fundamental currency for high performers. Your performance is grounded in the management of your energy.

People tend to do lots and lots of busywork to avoid the difficult and critical stuff. A better strategy is to do the difficult stuff right away and eliminate everything else.

> *"Doing something unimportant well does not make it important, neither does the fact that it takes a long time."*
> ~ Tim Ferriss

Chances are if you aren't doing something, it's not a priority. Be honest with yourself.

Try this exercise: Next time you want to use the words "I'm too busy," instead, insert the words "it's just not a priority."

The next time your son wants to play catch up with you, say, "Sorry, it's not a priority right now for me to play catch" or to your daughter the next time she asks for you to spend time with her, "Sorry honey, it's just not a priority right now."

See how that feels for a moment. See how your priorities quickly shift.

Prioritize what is important. Don't use busy as the default crutch in your life.

Mary Jean Arian wrote, "Gift from a Hair Dryer," and somehow, it kind of captures what a precious thing life is and to prioritize the people that are important to me:

> *Comb and dry. Comb and dry. 'Soon, I won't be able to do this anymore,' you say to yourself knowing that the little straight bob must inevitably yield to grown up coiffures and ugly curlers. What will she be like at 14? Where will her hair be blowing then—at 16 and 18? Do you suppose boys will love to watch her hair blow as you do now? And some of them will feel it on their faces. And one of them will marry her and her hair will be spread under the veil, and then, spread out on his pillow.*
> *And oh, you hate him a little and wonder where he is at this moment, whether he'll be good to her. They will grow old together. And the gold-brown hair*

will be gray. And you will be gone. And then, she will be gone—this very hair, that now your fingers smooth. And all the tears of the world swim for a second in your eyes as you snatch the plug out of the socket suddenly, and gather her into your arms, burying your face in the warm hair, as if you could seal this moment against all time.

Schedule your values. Prioritize what is most important to you. Good time management doesn't mean you do more; it means you do more of what really matters most. The difference between the values you hold and the life you live equals, or matches, the frustration you experience. Identify and hold fast to your non-negotiables, which means they go on the calendar first. Invest your best in what matters most.

Eliminate noise, embrace Sabbath

We have so much noise in our lives. Do you have a cell phone? Do you have email? Instagram? Snapchat? Facebook? Do you have a TV? Do you have more than one TV?

In the age of technological advances and the rise of social media, we are engaged with even more noise and distractions in our life. Why are we so attracted to noise? Why are we so repelled by the idea of silence? What is it about silence that is so difficult? How much noise do I voluntarily subject myself to?

I read about a guy who records nature sounds for film and television. He said that in 1968, in order to get one hour of undisturbed natural sound, like no airplanes, no cars…it would take him about 15 hours of recording time. He said that today, in order to get that same one hour of undisturbed sound, it takes him 2000 hours of recording time.

Do you find yourself exhausted from being subjected to the noise around you? Those who are parents, do you find that there isn't enough time in the day? Do you feel emotionally, psychologically, physically, and spiritually depleted? Maybe you are tapped out from trying to raise your kids or taking care of your elderly parents.

Those who are trying to climb the ladder of success? Do you find yourself exhausted, fatigued, overscheduled, overcommitted, and overworked? Maybe you think these are signs that you are an important person. You say to yourself, "I must be worth something. I must be climbing the ladder. My existence is validated, because I lead an exhausting, insanely paced life."

In the era where noise and distraction are constantly nipping at our heels for our attention, we must embrace other means to rejuvenate and recover.

Sometimes we need to get away, embrace boredom. Embrace recovery. Embrace idle time. Eliminate the noise around us.

Hugh Prather wrote a poem that shook me awake...

If I had only forgotten future greatness, and looked at the green things and the buildings, and reached out to those around me, and smelled the air, and ignored the forms and the self-styled obligations, and heard the rain on the roof, and put my arms around my wife. And it's not too late.

We need time to be bored. Time to notice the mundane. Time to get away, to free the mind from the chatter and noise around us. Time to focus on what really matters in life. Doing this actually makes us better!

As the essayist and cartoonist, Tim Kreider, once wrote, as he describes the importance of retreating away from the world of busyness:

Idleness is not just a vacation, an indulgence or a vice; it is as indispensable to the brain as vitamin D is to the body, and deprived of it we suffer a mental affliction as disfiguring as rickets...it is, paradoxically, necessary to getting any work done.

There is incredible value for you as you aim for downtime. The downtime provides you chances for new insights and revitalizes your energy level.

We must intentionally and deliberately create boundaries, identifying areas in our life where we are thoughtful about getting rest. Where we have stopping points in our day(s). Deliberate time for restoration. Unhurried time for rest.

In his book, *Sabbath*, Wayne Muller says it so brilliantly:

The busier we are the more important we seem to ourselves and, we imagine, to others. To be unavailable to our friends and family, to be unable to find time for the sunset, to whiz through our obligations without time for mindful breath, this has become the model of a successful life.

We have lost connection, Muller suggests. When we carve out time for Sabbath, we are reminded that we are human beings, *not* human doings. We need a healthy rhythm between work and life to maintain the Sabbath in our life. When we don't take time for restoration, we miss the opportunity to rejuvenate and reengage. As the psalmist says in Psalms twenty-three, "He makes me lie down in green pastures; He leads me beside still waters. He restores my soul."

> *"Sabbath gives the world the energy it*
> *needs to exist another six days."*
> ~ Abraham Joshua Heschel

Optimize simplicity

How do you optimize simplicity? How do you move from reactive to creative? One idea is to do your creative work FIRST thing in the morning. Don't do emails first. That's reactive work.

Eliminate the volume of information. A wealth of information leads to a poverty of attention. Consider that your attention is one of the most valuable assets you have...resulting in and making space for happiness and flourishing.

Author Winifred Gallagher suggests that our brains construct our worldview based on what *we pay attention to*. Based on research, he suggests that, *"who you are, what you think, feel, and do, what you love—is the sum of what you focus on."* Your world or your life is the outcome of what you pay attention to. The most effective individuals are the ones who aptly focus their attention.

Consider for a moment the type of mental world assembled when you commit significant time to focused endeavors.

Bottom line: Be willing to be bored. What that means is that we don't need to take out the smartphone and peruse it every few seconds and minutes of the day. Be okay with NOT having constant information. Starve the desire for constant stimulation and distraction. Embrace idle time.

Constantly vying for information and stimulation is like BF Skinner's rat test. For example: random reinforcement and anticipation of email. We have been compulsively trained to look and push for email and social media (e.g., Twitter, Facebook, etc.) updates.

Again, a wealth of information leads to a poverty of attention.

Focus on the fundamentals. Execute and iterate the fundamentals. World-class performers are less about complexity and more about optimizing simplicity.

The secret to genius is optimizing simplicity. If not, we become addicted to distraction. We try to maximize all these great opportunities and are then average at many things.

University College of London found in their research that it takes 21 days to instill a new habit…but it takes 66 days to reach it automatically.

We must stick with new habits and routines.

Most change is tough at the beginning, messy in the middle, and magnificent at the end. If a new habit or routine isn't hard and messy at the beginning, then it is not real change.

Clarity breeds mastery

Get clarity around what you want in your life. Clarity breeds mastery. Vague visions lead to vague executions. Most people spend more time on vacation planning than they do on planning their life.

Look more broadly at your life, not just at the habits and routines, and see how to optimize simplicity in your life. Also look at the big rocks and where you want to make the biggest accomplishments.

CALL TO ACTION

What are the 3 to 5 biggest things you want to accomplish in your life?

"Son, when you were born you cried while the world rejoiced. Live your life in such a way that when you die the world cries while you rejoice."
~ Robin Sharma

Create margin

We have forgotten to create and build MARGIN into our lives. We have forgotten to set up boundaries.

Margin is something we have to be deliberate and intentional about fighting for. In fact, it doesn't just happen.

In his book, *Margin: Restoring Emotional, Physical, Financial, and Time Reserves to Overloaded Lives*, Richard Swenson, M.D., defines margin like this:

> *Margin is the space between our load and our limits. It is the amount allowed beyond that which is needed. It is something held in reserve for contingencies or unanticipated situations. Margin is the gap between rest and exhaustion, the space between breathing freely and suffocating.*

Chances are when you hear the word "margin," your defenses come up. You may be thinking, "Ted, you have no idea how MUCH I have to get done! I don't have time to create and build margin into my life."

Frankly, now more than ever, we need to be intentional when investing in ourselves—adding margin. The stress in today's marketplace has increased exponentially. Carving out *margin* is more important than ever.

No Margin = Loss of Passion.
No Margin = Ineffectiveness.
No Margin = Lackluster Life and Leadership.

You need margin to bring some sort of balance to your life. You need margin to refuel your life. You need margin for setting priorities. You need margin to resurrect a dying vision. Most critically, you need margin to reflect and rejuvenate.

You know how in airplanes, there's the safety warning before take-off? What does it tell you? Put the oxygen mask on yourself first, before putting on someone else. Why should you put your mask on first? Because it's only THEN you can help others. (If you're not breathing anymore, you're not going to be all that helpful to others.)

Creating margin in your life allows you to "put your mask on first," which in turn allows you to be more helpful to others.

You're not able to contribute your best self if you're not taking care of yourself. You must prioritize and create better margin in order to help others.

It's not self-centered to carve out pockets of margin in your life. In fact, you are doing your family and friends, your organization, others, and yourself an injustice if you DON'T.

Below are suggested ideas and examples to consider when building margin into your life:

1. Learn to say yes to "less" and no to "more." (That means in areas where you are able to choose, consider the implications before saying yes.)

2. Invest in yourself. What other context can you leverage for the

purpose of rejuvenation and growth? (Examples: reading, podcasts, conferences.)

3. Use your benefit time at work. What a great opportunity to regain focus and clarity by setting aside time to get away.

4. Hit pause from work, especially on your days off...REST. (Don't check your iPhone every 20 seconds. Even your iPhone needs moments of R&R.)

5. Remember that you can't please everyone. You will disappoint some people. You can't be all things to all people. Hebert Swope says it best: "I cannot give you the formula for success, but I can give you the formula for failure—which is: try to please everyone."

6. Reduce meeting times and frequency. It forces you to plan ahead, and it makes the time you do spend in meetings more valuable.

7. Schedule the important activities. These are activities that contribute to your personal and professional goals and priorities.

Your life has poetic possibilities jammed with unending potential... with that comes the voice of wisdom saying, "slow down to create and build margin into your life."

WHEN LIFE, LEADERSHIP, AND BUSYNESS COLLIDE

"Our greatest fear should not be of failure but of succeeding at things in life that don't really matter."
~ F. Chan

Every time one of my sons has reached his next birthday, it is a reminder that I've been given another year and another extraordinary opportunity to lead and contribute to shaping my sons' lives. They are adventurous boys, with big hearts, who have a bright future and a world awaiting them...filled with unending possibilities.

As a dad, I'm definitely *learning in the wobble*. I've found that in the midst of my mistakes there are principles and (hidden) truths that yield nuggets of wisdom. A few years ago, before another son's first birthday, I found that I was succumbing to busyness and a hurried life.

Do you ever feel like life has been put in high gear, moving faster and faster? Do you feel like you have no time for things that are important to you? Do you have a hard time being present and enjoying the moment, instead focusing on what happened in the past or what could happen in the future?

Each of us can be intoxicated by busyness. We have mechanisms and systems in our society that help us move faster. Hurrying and busyness can even become a workaholics "badge of honor."

As mentioned in chapter 2, an American cardiologist, Meyer Friedman, says, in our society, we suffer from what he calls *hurry sickness*. The disease called *hurry sickness* suppresses our effectiveness and ability to be present in the moment. His antidote is that we have to give up on certain opportunities in order to take advantage of other ones. You can't answer every request. You can't please every voice. You are finite. You have limits.

Every day, every moment, every second transmits with it its own finality. Time is our one undeniably nonrenewable resource. "Where did the time go?" we ask when we sense we have spent the years wrongly or have taken some great gift, life, or family for granted. And the answer, of course, is that it went to the same place it always has. At the end of every day, one more box in the calendar has been moved from the future column to the past column, from possibility to history.

The reality is if we don't properly align our priorities and treasure our time, someone else will. We must be ruthless in setting up the appropriate boundaries to ensure others aren't dictating our priorities.

Those you care about the most deserve your best.

As leaders, one of the practices I recommend is intentionally pausing for a moment to consider the current landscape of your life. What initiatives, projects, and other activities are you involved in? What commitments have you made? What is your "yes-to-no" ratio?

One author suggests the following remedy for living a hurried, fast-paced life…change of pace + change of place = change of perspective.

While I'm an advocate of such practices of evaluation, I find myself being an offender of *not* taking my own advice. A few years ago, I was incredibly overextended. I felt internally (don't ignore your instincts) that it was time to slow down for a season, in order to focus on what was important in life.

I ended up relinquishing several leadership responsibilities, one with a nonprofit organization I had been leading for years. I also put a hold on teaching at a local university, and I bowed out of board responsibilities. Additionally, I stopped side collaborative projects for a season.

Why?

Because it was a season where I was overextending myself. I found myself "hurrying" more, and being "present" less for those who were most important to me. I knew it was time to create margin and put boundaries in place.

Much of my decision to relinquish commitments and set clear priorities in my life was a result of reading the story of Eugene O'Kelly, a former CEO of KPMG, one of the largest accounting firms in the world. As CEO, his calendar was booked 18 months in advance. Working 12 to 15 hours a day, he had an insanely busy life. He embodied the essence of what some would call an unhealthy balance of busyness.

All of it came to a screeching halt after he was diagnosed at the age of 53 with advanced stages of brain cancer. He was given three months to live.

For the next 90 days, he tried to create what O'Kelly called *perfect moments*: an experience with others when time stands still for a moment. A moment where you are fully present, where you leave the past behind and set aside the future, and fully engage in the present.

You might be thinking right now, "Ted, what does this have to do with leadership?" Frankly, it has a lot to do with leadership. It is choosing to align your life in such a way that you balance your life and create margin for those people/things that are important. Choosing to be present in the moment. Hitting the pause button to enjoy those perfect moments.

"Why do they not teach you that life is a finger snap and an eye blink, and that you should not allow a moment to pass you by without taking joyous, ecstatic note of it, not wasting a single moment of its swift, breakneck circuit?"
~ Pat Conroy

This weekend I'm hitting the pause button, soaking in the gift I have been given with my four sons (aka cowboys). They are reminders to me that living a hurried life is for amateurs. That leadership is found in ruthlessly and continuously eliminating hurry from one's life.

CALL TO ACTION

How are you doing these days when it comes eliminating hurry? What could you do this week to make a strong commitment to say "yes to less," and "no to more?" How could that change your life, family, and leadership?

the ROAD of
COMFORT
is
OVER-
CROWDED
these days

Chapter 8
Train Yourself Every Day

Train Yourself: Choose to Be Great Every Day

Train yourself to be great. Don't misunderstand me…the greatness I speak of isn't necessarily scoring the winning shot, knocking your presentation out of the park, getting the dream job, or other examples similar to this.

Greatness can be found in the daily routine things that we train ourselves to notice, to pay attention to, and to intentionally live out. Many times greatness can be seen in the mundane and the trivial circumstances we face every day.

We have the opportunity to make small decisions that have a big impact (on ourselves and others), that have a ripple effect on the sea of human life.

Below are over 20 thought-provoking considerations that can be integrated into your life, maybe taking one each day to practice and train yourself. Some of these can be mastered in a day, while others might take longer. In either case, the following are challenges to strive towards to live the best version of yourself!

Challenge 1: Today's challenge is to "go FIRST..."

Smile, first

Apologize, first

Say hi, first

Forgive, first

Be generous, first

Encourage, first

There's power in going first.

Challenge 2: Every day is a MIRACLE.

Every day is a MIRACLE.

Every day has two miraculous moments. The first is the moment you wake up and realize you have been given another chance at life. The second is the moment before you go to sleep and realize you get to put whatever mistakes you've made behind you.

The question for you is, "when you wake up tomorrow, what will you do differently?" How would you serve those around you differently and leverage your strengths in the service of something beyond yourself?

Every day is a miracle. Every day. Treat it as such.

Your life is an echo of the miraculous.

Today matters. Make it count.

Challenge 3: Forgive others

Forgiveness is a decision, not an emotion. It's your decision.

Forgive others. Forgive quickly. Don't allow others stuff, and maybe even their shortcomings, to stop you from forgiving. Don't hold a grudge. Don't lay hold on the tantalizing lure of resentment. It's a trap.

Not forgiving others is holding others hostage in a prison in your own mind and heart. Be careful of the prison of resentment, where you wish bad things on others. As the brilliant Fredrick Buechner so eloquently penned:

> *Of all the deadly sins, resentment appears to be the most fun. To lick your wounds and savor the pain you will give back is in many ways a feast fit for a king. But then it turns out that what you are eating at the banquet of bitterness is your own heart. The skeleton at the feast is you. You start out holding a grudge, but in the end the grudge holds you.*

We have a choice. When we forgive, we set others free from the little prison we have placed in our mind for holding others captive.

Choose not to give into the whims of retaliation.

You have the choice. Retaliation or mercy. Prison or freedom. Hatred or grace.

You have a choice to make. If you don't forgive, forget and go forward, you will retain, remember, and regress.

Choose wisely.

Forgive.

Challenge 4: Powerful phrases to remember

I was perusing some of my old journals the other day and found these powerful phrases to remember.

Powerful (simple) phrases to use in our everyday language:

- I believe in you.
- I'm proud of you.
- I trust you.
- I respect you.
- I'm sorry.
- I love you.

Equally important to remember is that there is *nothing* wrong with saying:

- I don't know.
- I don't understand.

- I think I've messed up.
- I need help.

Challenge 5: Your gifts and conventional wisdom

"We don't rise to the level of our expectations [challenge],
we fall to the level of our training."
~ Archilochus

What do you have in you? A seed of incredible possibility and potential. Inside of you there is a well of underdeveloped budding resources waiting to be exploited.

I believe that every person who reads this has untapped abilities within. Pursue the untouched treasures that reside in you, which need to be developed. There is a giant inside of you. There is a goldmine of genius waiting to be maximized.

Don't be trapped by a culture that tries to define you by titles or its own expectations. For example, many will try to put guardrails on you by defining you by a title. You're an engineer. You're a programmer. You're a stay-at-home parent. Once we buy into the titles that others give us, we may be tempted to no longer seek what could be, and what should be, which is our extraordinary life.

Refuse to allow others to put a period on your life and define you; instead, your life is a series of commas. Pursue and develop the treasure within.

We have a seed inside each of us, and one of your aims in life should be to use your time wisely and produce what's in the seed. The notion that there is only one tree in the seed is a myth…there could be a forest waiting to grow.

Allow your life to evolve into something beyond titles, job descriptions and others expectations of you. There is a seed of greatness inside you. Focus on the seed, which in turn can produce a tree, which in turn can produce a forest.

There is a forest of possibilities waiting to flourish.

Challenge 6: Be around those who make you better

Who you spend time with will dictate who you will become.

> *"You are the sum total of the 5 people you hang around the most."*
> ~ Jim Rohn

People don't value what they don't fight for. Remember, the purpose of any goal is NOT achieving. It's WHO you are becoming in the process. And who you surround yourself with will bring out the best version of you.

Challenge 7: Personal board of directors

While navigating the spectrum of life's high and lows, we all need help. We all need people who dole out words of wisdom and insights that will help us in our decision points. In fact, years ago, one of the greatest bits of advice I ever got was to ask a few wise, trusted people in my life to be kind of a personal board of directors for me.

"Can you speak wisdom into my life? Here's what I'm thinking. If you were me, what would you do or consider?"

Almost all train wreck decisions (and we all make them) could be prevented just by asking and seeking input from a personal "board of directors."

Everybody needs a personal board of directors: a handful of men or women whom you trust to give wise counsel. Quit trying to figure out everything on your own. Get around people whose character you admire and trust, who have good judgment, who love you, and who are FOR you. Then: LISTEN. Be open to the wisdom they share. Be coachable. As proverbs suggest, "The way of fools seems right to them, but the wise listen to advice."

Challenge 8: Focusing on appreciating

"Remove your expectation for appreciation."
~ Tony Robbins

Appreciate others. Focus on others.

When people are suffering they are many times obsessing about self. Move from obsessing over self and start appreciating others.

Every day plant good seeds, regardless of your mood. You bring your own weather to the picnic. Make someone's day, every day.

You need to pause for applause. Appreciate the good things happening around you in your life. Recognize the bright spots that are all around you that are yearning to be noticed and called out. Problems will always be present, but that doesn't mean you shouldn't celebrate and appreciate the bright spots. As Chip and Dan Heath suggest, from their book, *Switch*, "Instead of being archeological problem solvers, we should be bright spot finders."

Challenge 9: The awesome jar

On our kitchen counter at home sits our "AWESOME JAR." It's just a mason jar that we use to celebrate the good things in our day. Whenever something good happens, something that brings us JOY, one of us will write it down on a slip of paper and add it to the jar. You'd think we'd remember all these great things, but somehow we forget. This "AWESOME" Jar is a like our "remember the good" and "what's going well" Jar.

Find a container and make it your family's AWESOME Jar. Make it a habit to add one thing each day. If it was a bad day and you can't think of anything, then write, "We are all still alive today!" The more good you notice today, the more you will notice tomorrow.

Take time throughout the year to review the notes you've put in the jar, and I promise, they will bring you JOY! It's awesome.

Challenge 10: Pursue discomfort and embrace the suck

Get comfortable with being uncomfortable. Motivation is different that mental toughness. Navy Seals seek out pain. Seek discomfort instead of avoiding it.

If you are not doing anything that scares you or challenges you in such a way that you're unsure of yourself…then you've outgrown yourself. If your everyday challenges are so predictable that they require nothing of you beyond what you did yesterday, then you're not growing.

Pursuing discomfort may not seem natural, but it is critical.

Discomfort brings change.

Embrace the suck and challenge yourself.

The road of comfort is overcrowded these days and seldom brings you to a place of growth.

Your growth depends on your pursuing discomfort.

That's where growth happens.

Challenge 11: Joy can be present, in spite of pain

Consider a character in a movie that faces NO challenges or adversity…if that was the case, you would have NO movie. There has to be conflict, adversity, and hardship. The only way we can change in life is by facing hard times. Yes, hard times. Joy is what we experience many times after we face challenges and adversity…transformation many times happens in those heat experiences, in the furnace of adversity.

Sometimes joy is the byproduct of work.

Consider the challenges you have faced, are currently facing, or will face. The harder something is to attain, the more you value it in life.

You are not a victim of life's circumstances. Victims have a high level of locus of control (blaming everything on someone else). A victim is someone who has NO power. That's NOT you.

Adversity can be turned into an advantage. A stumbling block can turn into a steppingstone.

Learn to train yourself to see the other side of pain, adversity, and challenge. The other side renders growth within ourselves and contribution beyond ourselves.

Challenge 12: You will experience setbacks when pursuing your dreams

Keep moving forward. Keep building. Keep creating. Keep designing. Keep writing. Keep composing. Keep iterating.

Challenge 13: Your heart matters

"Awake my son!"
~ Psalmist

To my sons and to many of you reading this, your heart really matters. The greatest gift I can give to you is to KNOW that your heart really matters. It matters a lot. Your heart is a living treasure…not to be buried so that forty years later you have to go on an archeological dig to try and uncover it.

Challenge 14: What should I write on a billboard?

Someone asked me the other day what would I write on a billboard? The word "Now." Be present now. Start now. Be kind now. Pursue your dreams now. Take action now.

Challenge 15: Critics, trolls, and pig-wrestling

"To avoid criticism, do nothing, say nothing, and be nothing."
~ Aristotle

We all know individuals, who, if a position existed within a company for professional criticizers, would be top-performers year after year. Sometimes they excuse their knack for negativity as a "wiring" issue or some other euphemism.

None of us are *immune* to negative criticism. This type of criticism can hurt deeply and unfortunately, there isn't a "no criticism" pill you can take. (Keep in mind, I'm not speaking of constructive criticism, which has tremendous value for growth and learning.)

It's easy to have "less than holy" thoughts towards the people who criticize in a *destructive* manner. The more personal the criticism and the deeper the dig, the worse we feel toward them. We can have this almost instinctive response of retaliation. However, getting "even" is futile. It takes up worthless mind-space entertaining thoughts of retaliation. The reality is that most people who are negative about you and others are usually not happy with *themselves*, and not happy with where they are in life.

People do what they do because of who they are, not because of who you are.

I will encourage you to avoid the vortex of the *negative* critic. If you get sucked in, the critic's words can elicit a storm of anger within you and make you want to pursue retaliation for the wrong you perceived they caused. Giving in to anger hurts you more than the critic. As Mark Twain said:

Anger is an acid that can do more harm to the vessel in which it is stored than to anything on which it is poured.

You can effectively deliver a punishment to a negative critic by not responding to them. That's right…don't respond.

I have found that the best response to negative criticism is to "starve it of oxygen"—don't give it a response. Responding drives attention to it and often causes further negativity on both sides. A wise person once said:

Don't wrestle with pigs. You both get filthy…but the pigs like it.

Author, uber-blogger, and speaker Seth Godin says that critics are like trolls. He says, "Trolls are critics who gain perverse pleasure in relentlessly tearing you and your ideas down." He goes on to point out that:

1. Trolls will always be trolling.
2. Critics rarely create.
3. They live in a tiny echo chamber, ignored by everyone except the trolled and the other trolls.
4. Professionals (that's you) get paid to ignore them. It's part of your job.

Godin goes on to say, "'Can't please everyone' isn't just an aphorism, it's the secret of being remarkable."

One of the secrets to being REMARKABLE is to focus on impact, not approval.

Challenge 16: Remember these three things

Simple, but easy to remember.

1. Do the right thing.
2. Do the best you can.
3. Show people you care.

Challenge 17: Character matters

Commit to being a person of strong character.

Our character is revealed during highs and lows.

Show humility in the mountain top experiences.

Be diligent, focused, and steadfast in the valleys.

The in-between spaces…commit to be faithful.

Character matters.

Challenge 18: Don't sit in the driver's seat of "what ifs"

There is more risk in doing nothing than in taking risks. Playing it "safe" can be risky.

You should be more afraid of missing an opportunity than failing.

Don't lie in the bed of "what ifs…" Instead, live a life of "oh wells," not "what ifs."

Quit looking in the rearview mirror. The rearview mirror is so little and the windshield (in front of you) is so BIG. Spend more time looking forward than looking backward.

Reflect (looking back), yes. Remaining stuck looking back, no.

Challenge 19: Take ownership

There's empowerment when we take ownership for something. We can accept things as they are or change them.

Never allow your inability to do everything to undermine your determination to do something. Even if it's one small act. Never underestimate the power of one small act.

"The most common way people give up their power is by thinking they don't have any."
~ Alice Malsenior Walker

Challenge 20: Stop waiting to be picked, choose yourself.

"Pick me, pick me" acknowledges the power of the system and passes responsibility to someone else to initiate. Even worse, "pick me, pick me" moves the blame from you to them. (If you don't get picked, it's their fault, not yours.).

Far too many of us end up feeling as if our lives just happened rather than that our lives were what we CHOSE to happen.

Reject the tyranny of the chosen and picked. Choose yourself. Pick yourself.

Challenge 21: Path #1 or path #2

Princeton philosopher Walter Kaufmann coined the word *decidopho-*

bia. He noticed that human beings are afraid of making decisions. We don't want the anxiety that goes along with the possibility of being wrong. We can become paralyzed by the choices in front of us.

Choosing scares us, but there is also a thrill and excitement to it. Poet Archibald MacLeish has said, *"What is freedom? Freedom is the right to choose: the right to create for oneself the alternative of choice. Without the possibility of choice a man is not a man but a member, an instrument, a thing."*

Choosing involves a process:

- Seeing the opportunity
- Identifying your options
- Assessing and evaluating
- Making a decision
- Learning from that decision.

Challenge 22: Try firing bullets, then cannonballs

Consider Jim Collins recommendation of firing bullets first, then cannonballs. Firing bullets looks like making small choices, decisions, to gain empirical validation before making a big decision (firing cannonballs).

Collins brilliantly suggests:

> *First, you fire bullets (low-cost, low-risk, low-distraction experiments) to figure out what will work—calibrating your line of sight by taking small shots. Then, once you have empirical validation, you fire a cannonball (concentrating resources into a big bet) on the calibrated line of sight. Calibrated cannonballs correlate with outsized results; uncalibrated cannonballs correlate with disaster. The ability to turn small proven ideas (bullets) into huge hits (cannonballs) counts more than the sheer amount of pure innovation.*

Challenge 23: Stop waiting for a roadmap and follow the compass

Quit waiting for signs. Bread crumbs are all around you. Start picking them up and moving forward.

Stop waiting for a roadmap from life and follow the compass.

Challenge 24: Stop living like an amateur

What ails many of us is that we can acquiesce to a life of an amateur.

You must train yourself to rise above mediocrity, to live up to your full potential and to live as you were born to live.

"Leaders [that's YOU] must challenge the process. Precisely because any system will unconsciously conspire to maintain the status quo and prevent change."
~ The Leadership Challenge

Rising to your potential requires you to challenge even the status quo within you. A shift in thinking. A growth mindset. To change your mind. Rising will require you to give up a life of comfort.

Self-discipline is a must. Sacrifice is required. The ability is there.

It's time for you to RISE.

Stop waiting for all your ducks to get in a row before you take action.

Take action.

The ability is there.

You can quench the fire inside of you by refusing to act.

Drive yourself.

Put your best into each day.

Be mentally attentive.

Don't be the person who has a million ideas and says I will start tomorrow. Remember, there are seven days in a week and tomorrow is not one of them.

A final reminder: You WILL...

You will hit roadblocks. Remember, obstacles and adversity are moments to experience growth.

You will have moments to quit and run. Show up anyway and stay committed for the long haul.

You will have moments of glorious wins and highs. Don't show off. Stay humble.

You will have moments of defeat. Stay strong.

You will make mistakes. Treat yourself with grace.

You will have failures. Reflect. Learn. Get back in the game.

You will have moments to rise and be strong. Rise. Be strong.

You will have moments to be kind to others, especially your enemies. Show kindness.

You will have moments to sit down and shrink back in fear. Stand up and move forward. Act in the face of fear.

You will have moments where you will thirst for others validation. Self-validate.

You will have moments to commit to learning a new skill. Dedicate and focus on mastering the skill and techniques necessary.

You will have moments to reinvent yourself. Become better, reinvent.

You will have moments where pride and arrogance will want to seep in. Ask for help.

You will have moments where truth needs to be spoken. Courageously and boldly speak truth.

You will have times where you will want to hold on to things and possessions. Give generously.

You will have moments when you feel your title, position, and career define you. They don't. Remember that you are more than your title, position, and career. You are a child of God. You are made in His image.

You will have moments when fear will want to define you and hold you back. Be brave and courageous in spite of fear.

You will have defining moments to live out your values, though not popular. Live out your values with conviction.

You will have moments where your gut says to go right and others say go left. Go right, courageously. Learn. Grow. Repeat.

You will have moments, every day, to stand in awe and wonder. Pause. Stand in awe and wonder.

You will have moments, every day, to show appreciation to others. Stop. No, seriously stop what you are doing. Be grateful. Show appreciation for others.

An envoi or envoy is a short stanza at the end of a poem used either to address an imagined or actual person. It was medieval tradition that there would be a small poem at the end of a long poem or book, called an envoi (French origin). This was the opportunity for the poet to say goodbye to his poem or book and wish it along its way with hopes that the poem or book might bring the readers some benefit.

Go, little book,
out of this house and into the world,
carriage made of paper rolling toward town
bearing a single passenger
beyond the reach of this jittery pen
and far from the desk and the nosy gooseneck lamp.
It is time to decamp,
put on a jacket and venture outside,
time to be regarded by other eyes,
bound to be held in foreign hands.
So off you go, infants of the brain,
with a wave and some bits of fatherly advice:
stay out as late as you like,
don't bother to call or write,
and talk to as many strangers as you can.

~ Aimless Love, Billy Collins

Acknowledgments

I felt an enormous sense of accomplishment when I finished this book. It was one of the most challenging projects I have ever taken on. The completion of this book was a result of the tremendous love, support and encouragement from family and friends. Thank you for standing by me. I hope I make you proud.

Here's a list of people (some I know and some I don't know) who have inspired me in one way or another:

Parker Palmer, Warren Buffett, Benjamin Franklin, Anne Lamott, Brene Brown, Simon Sinek, Howard Hendricks, Derek Sivers, Julia Child, Corey Criswell, Timothy Ferriss, Susan Rooks, Zig Ziglar, Guy Kawasaki, Mark Hoeft, Steve Sample, Howard Schultz, Chris Anderson, J.K. Rowling, John D. Rockefeller, Steve Jobs, Ryan Delahanty, Eugene O'Kelly, John Maxwell, Scott Belsky, Kevin Kull, Randolph Hearst, Emily Viviani, Walt Disney, Michael Jordan, Kurt Lewin, Tom Berliner, Jim Kouzes, Barry Posner, Ryan Anderson, Vince Lombardi, Ed Saloga, Andy Stanley, Jeff Bezos, Sarah Letendre, Ryan Higley.

And of course, Kathryn, George, Clark, Paul, and Luke. And my mom and dad, who always believed in me to bring the best out of those around me.

About the Author

Ted W. Egly is a speaker, writer, outdoorsman, adventure race fanatic, and experienced leader. He has a passion for teaching people how to take action in spite of our fears, how to keep going when we want to quit, and how to be present in the moments that matter most. His solutions are born from his experience, from fascinating connections he makes to the world of science, technology, leadership, and fatherhood, and from a life spent pushing the boundaries physically and mentally. He's constantly reinventing himself: from a childhood spent battling a life-threatening illness, to working with the Billionaire, to working with a Chicago-based telecommunications company, father to four sons, and well-respected leader in one of the foremost executive education organizations in the world. He has a BA in Organizational Management and an MBA in Human Resource Management and Organizational Leadership, both from Aurora University, Dunham Graduate School of Business.

Made in the USA
Columbia, SC
26 September 2019